WHEN A
MAN
LOVES A
WOMAN

D1502521

WHEN A MAN LOVES A WOMAN

pursuing her heart

JAMES FORD JR.

MOODY PUBLISHERS
CHICAGO

© 2004, 2012 by
JAMES FORD JR.

All rights reserved. No part of this book may be reproduced in any form without permission in writing from the publisher, except in the case of brief quotations embodied in critical articles or reviews.

All Scripture quotations, unless otherwise indicated, are taken from the King James Version.

Scripture quotations marked NKJV are taken from the *New King James Version*. Copyright © 1982, 1992 by Thomas Nelson, Inc. Used by permission. All rights reserved.

Scripture quotations marked NIV are taken from the *Holy Bible, New International Version*®. NIV®. Copyright © 1973, 1978, 1984 by Biblica, Inc.™ Used by permission of Zondervan. All rights reserved worldwide. www.zondervan.com

Scripture quotations marked NASB are taken from the *New American Standard Bible*®, Copyright © 1960, 1962, 1963, 1968, 1971, 1972, 1973, 1975, 1977, 1995 by The Lockman Foundation. Used by permission. (www.Lockman.org)

Edited by Cynthia Ballenger
Interior design: Ragont Design
Cover design: Brand Navigation LLC
Cover images: iStockphoto.com

Library of Congress Cataloging-in-Publication Data

Ford, James, 1951-
    When a man loves a woman: pursuing her heart / by James Ford, Jr.
        p. cm.
    Includes bibliographical references
    ISBN 978-0-8024-6838-3
    1. Men—Religious Life. 2. Love—Religious Aspects—Christianity.
    3. Men-women relationships—Religious aspects—Christianity. I. Title.

    BV4440.F67 2004
    248.8'425—dc22   2004009699

We hope you enjoy this book from Moody Publishers. Our goal is to provide high-quality, thought-provoking books and products that connect truth to your real needs and challenges. For more information on other books and products written and produced from a biblical perspective, go to www.moodypublishers.com or write to:

Moody Publishers
820 N. LaSalle Boulevard
Chicago, IL 60610

7 9 10 8

Printed in the United States of America

R0463586124

This book is dedicated to my wife, Leslie Ann Ford.
She is my "12th" Rose and the inspiration behind the writing of it.
She is my faithful friend, loyal confidante, dutiful wife,
loving mother, extraordinary grandmother,
and the sole object of my affection. I thank God for her.

JACOB WENT on his journey and came to the land of the people of the East. And he looked, and saw a well in the field; and behold, there were three flocks of sheep lying by it; for out of that well they watered the flocks. A large stone was on the well's mouth. Now all the flocks would be gathered there; and they would roll the stone from the well's mouth, water the sheep, and put the stone back in its place on the well's mouth.

And Jacob said to them, "My brethren, where are you from?" And they said, "We are from Haran." Then he said to them, "Do you know Laban the son of Nahor?" And they said, "We know him." So he said to them, "Is he well?" And they said, "He is well. And look, his daughter Rachel is coming with the sheep."

Then he said, "Look, it is still high day; it is not time for the cattle to be gathered together. Water the sheep, and go and feed them." But they said, "We cannot until all the flocks are gathered together, and they have rolled the stone from the well's mouth; then we water the sheep."

Now while he was still speaking with them, Rachel came with her father's sheep, for she was a shepherdess. And it came to pass, when Jacob saw Rachel the daughter of Laban his mother's brother, and the sheep of Laban his mother's brother, that Jacob went near and rolled the stone from the well's mouth, and watered the flock of Laban his mother's brother. Then Jacob kissed Rachel, and lifted up his voice and wept. And Jacob told Rachel that he was her father's relative and that he was Rebekah's son. So she ran and told her father.

Then it came to pass, when Laban heard the report about Jacob his sister's son, that he ran to meet him, and embraced him and kissed him, and brought him to his house. So he told Laban all these things. And Laban said to him, "Surely you are my bone and my flesh." And he stayed with him for a month. Genesis 29:1–14 NKJV

Contents

Introduction

THE FIRST ARTIST of "When a Man Loves a Woman," was not Michael Bolton as many young people believe. Actually it was written, produced, and recorded by two others before Michael was born. Percy Sledge arranged the familiar tune in 1966, but Jacob of the Old Testament penned the first version in the twenty-ninth chapter of Genesis.

Everyone knows that Jacob of the Old Testament was a rascal, a supplanter, and a deceiver, but Jacob knew how to do one thing very well . . . Jacob knew how to love a woman.

Jacob won Rachel's heart. He was willing to work and wait to wed the only woman he ever wanted. Finally, because of his sincere commitment to protect their love, Jacob warned Rachel.

If you are a baby boomer (born between 1946 and 1964) or older, you may remember Charles Boyer. He was the suave, dapper, handsome, and graceful leading man to some of the most famous and beautiful starlets of the silver screen. However, that persona was reserved for the camera and fan magazines. In real life, Charles loved only one woman: his wife, Patricia. Everyone who knew Charles and Pat maintained that they had a lifelong love affair. They were no less lovers, friends, and companions after forty-four years of marriage than they were in their first year together.

When Patricia developed liver cancer, Charles could not bear for her to know her true condition, so for six months he sat by her bedside day and night, providing hope and cheer. Patricia eventually died in his arms. Two days after her death, Charles died by his own hand. He left a note that read, "Her love was life to me. All I've ever wanted in life was Pat. Now she's gone and life has no more meaning."

Charles Boyer was a man upon whose words and movements millions of women were fixed. Yet, he was not interested in any other woman, because he was in love with his wife. Nothing could distract or dissuade him. Charles thought of no one else. Though the winds of time, sickness, and death blew hard enough to snatch his beloved from his arms, nothing could take her from his heart.

Although Charles Boyer's story is tragic, it shows how deeply this man loved his woman. Love your woman with everything you've got. You chose her because you knew she was the one for you—the one God gave especially to you to have, to hold, and to cherish for the rest of your lives. Love your wife as Christ loves the church and find balance showing your love for your woman even

When a Man Loves a Woman

in a death-related situation because of your surrender to the One who loves you unconditionally.

Men, I've written this book so that you can read it one section at a time and not feel bombarded by the information enclosed. If you digest it a little at a time, I guarantee that you will come away with a different perspective on life, love, and what God has been trying to tell you about how important it is to show your love for your woman.

Generally the man is the "thermostat" in the relationship and the woman is generally the "thermometer." He sets the temperature and she registers it. He is the initiator and she is the responder.

God made Adam first (Genesis 2:15) and placed him in the garden of Eden (his first "crib"). The Lord gave Adam three things in this order: (1) his work, (2) his word, (3) and then his wife. He was to be a gardener and a guardian who is a provider and a protector.

Truly Eve was in the mind of God before she was in the arms of Adam, and everything she needed was already provided before she ever came on the scene.

"Therefore shall a *man* leave his father and his mother, and shall cleave unto his wife: and they shall be one flesh" (Genesis 2:24, emphasis mine).

"*He who* finds a wife finds a good thing, and obtains favor from the Lord" (Proverbs 18:22 NKJV, emphasis mine).

I think this is further validated in the New Testament when Paul tells husbands to love their wives like Christ loved the church and gave Himself for it.

Christ initiated the unconditional relationship with the church. He sacrificed Himself! He sanctified her by the washing of the water by the Word! Ephesians 5:26 begins with "that," which is called a "resultant clause" in Greek. This means everything done prior to the statement was done to produce what comes after the statement. In other words, what Jesus did for the church resulted in her being presented to Him without spot or wrinkle. It was as if Jesus said, "the church is messed up; that's why I'll be her thermostat and I will roll up My sleeves and work on her to deal with all her imperfections so that she can be what I want her to be."

Christ didn't say the church is messed up so I need to find another one. Nor did He say the church is messed up; I need to divorce her. He said the church is messed up so I need to fix her up so I can have the kind of church that I want.

When unconditional love is the foundation of the relationship, the woman feels secure and significant. I think the story of John Blanchard perfectly illustrates my point.

John Blanchard stood up from the bench, straightened his Army uniform, and studied the crowd of people making their way through Grand Central Station. He looked for the girl whose heart

When a Man Loves a Woman

he knew, but whose face he didn't, the girl with the rose.

His interest in her had begun thirteen months before in a Florida library. Taking a book off the shelf, he found himself intrigued, not with the works of the book, but with the notes penciled in the margin. The soft handwriting reflected a thoughtful soul and insightful mind. In the front of the book, he discovered the previous owner's name.

With time and effort he located her address. She lived in New York City. He wrote her a letter introducing himself and inviting her to correspond. The next day he was shipped overseas for service in World War II. During the next year and one month, the two grew to know each other through the mail. Each letter was a seed falling on a fertile heart. A romance was budding.

Blanchard requested a photograph, but she refused. She felt that if he really cared, it wouldn't matter what she looked like.

When the day finally came for him to return from Europe, they scheduled their first meeting: 7:30 p.m. at Grand Central Station in New York. "You'll recognize me," she wrote, "by the red rose I'll be wearing on my coat."

I'll let Mr. Blanchard tell you what happened:

A young woman was coming toward me, her figure long and slim. Her blond hair lay back in curls from her delicate ears; her eyes were blue as flowers. Her lips and chin had a gentle firmness, and in her pale green suit she was like springtime come alive. I started toward her, entirely forgetting to notice that she was not wearing a rose. As I moved, a small, provocative smile curved her lips. "Going my way, sailor?" she murmured.

Almost uncontrollably I made one step closer to her, and then I saw Hollis Maynell.

She was standing almost directly behind the girl. A woman well past forty, she had graying hair tucked under a worn hat, her thick ankled feet thrust into low heeled shoes. The girl in the green suit was walking quickly away. I felt as though I was split in two, so keen was my desire to follow her, and yet so deep was my longing for the woman whose spirit had truly companioned me and upheld my own.

And there she stood. Her pale, plump face was gentle and sensible, her gray eyes had a warm and kindly twinkle. I did not hesitate. My finger gripped the small worn blue leather copy of the book that was to identify me to her. This would not be love, but it would be something precious, something perhaps even better than love, a friendship for which I had been and must ever be grateful.

I squared my shoulders and saluted and held out the book to the woman, even while I spoke I felt choked by the bitterness of my disappointment. "I'm Lieutenant John Blanchard, and you must be Miss Maynell. I am so glad you could meet me; may I take you to dinner?"

The woman's face broadened into a tolerant smile. "I don't know what this is all about, son," she answered, "but the young lady in the green suit who just went by, she begged me to wear this rose on my coat. And she said if you were to ask me out to dinner, I should go and tell you that she is waiting for you in a big restaurant across the street. She said it was some kind of test!"

Well, Jacob is a "John Blanchard" to Rachel. It is my sincere hope that Jacob's life will serve as a yardstick to assist married and single Christian men, in evaluating the length, breadth, width, and height of your love for the women you hold dear and to continue on after you marry. May the Lord give you comprehension of His Word as you prayerfully consider what the Scriptures have to say about what happens When a Man Loves a Woman.

Chapter One

when a
man
loves
a woman

a man and
his woman

BROTHERS, I'M SURE you remember the phenomenon we used to call a "house party." All evening long you got your groove on, dancing with any woman willing to dance with you—that is, until the end of the party. That last dance was always a slow one, played against a backdrop of dimmed lights and emotion, reserved for the one you loved or the one you wanted to love so you could dance so close it was too close, well . . .

I remember one occasion when I could hardly wait for the last dance. The lyrics of the current hit song "When a Man Loves a Woman," by Percy Sledge, would tell "Pug" (*pronounced Pudge*), also known as Leslie, the woman who would eventually become my wife, everything I had in my heart for her.

The song tells the story of a brother in love. He is totally pre-occupied. You know him! His nose is open. He can't think of anything or anyone else but her. There isn't anything he wouldn't do or sacrifice to be with her. She is wonderful! The sun, moon, stars, and planets all revolve around her. She's perfect. If he could change anything about her, he wouldn't, because she can do no wrong. If she did something wrong, he'd never notice. If anyone ever tried to bring her shortcomings to his attention, they'd run the risk of losing his friendship, since the woman he loved was perfect.

Nothing was too good for her. He'd spend all of his money on her. If she said, "Jump," he'd ask, "How high?" He begged her to treat him right, since he was totally and completely at her mercy.

"Don't play me!" he'd plead, because he knew she had the power and opportunity. If she ever decided to treat him bad, he'd be the very last to know, because he was so caught up in his feelings for her . . .

Someone once said, "Love is a feeling, and when you feel it, you feel like you've never felt before." Sometimes love just feels amorphous. It is beyond measure. Love can be demonstrated in many ways. Yet, its description and definition are elusive.

Pastor Crawford Loritts shared with us at a Pastors' Conference held at Moody Bible Institute his response to his son's question, "Dad, how do I know I'm in love?" His reply was, "Son, you

When a Man Loves a Woman

know you're in love, when you look at her like you look at my refrigerator!" (Moody Pastors' Conference, plenary session, 2000)

Dr. Gary Chapman defines love in the following manner: "love is two consonants, L+V; two vowels, O+E; two fools, you and me" (Moody Pastors' Conference, workshop, 1985). However you define it, love is a verb. "God so loved the world that He *gave . . .*" (John 3:16 NKJV, emphasis mine).

Throughout history men have gone to great lengths to demonstrate love. Real love will cause a man to behave in ways that he would not normally consider rational, just as the lyrics to "When a Man Loves a Woman" imply.

WHO'S THE WOMAN GOD HAS FOR YOU?

When I first saw Leslie forty years ago (when she was eight years old), I knew she would grow up and become my wife. I told her so the very first day I met her. Of course, I don't recommend that everyone propose to his intended the first time they meet, but I do believe that it is possible to recognize your life partner instantly.

The well was a regular place of work. It was neither extraordinary nor supernatural. Scripture reveals that it was customary for Rachel to go to the well to water her father's sheep.

It was in the course of her normal, daily activity that Jacob discovered Rachel. Rachel did not waste time peering into a pool of water at her reflection, daydreaming about a speculative suitor. Like Rachel, singles must diligently pursue and perfect the gifts, talents, ministry, and vocation that God has uniquely ordained for them. Second Peter 1:5–7 outlines the training sequence prescribed by God:

> Giving all diligence, add to your faith virtue; and to virtue knowledge; and to knowledge temperance; and to temperance patience; and to patience godliness; and to godliness brotherly kindness; and to brotherly kindness charity.

ADD TO YOUR FAITH

There are basic skills that every growing Christian should master—most notably, the ability to lead a person to Christ and encourage them to maturity. Others include teaching (2 Timothy 1:11), preaching (1 Timothy 2:7), counseling (2 Corinthians 1:4), and serving (Romans 1:1). However, genuine ministry and unearthing God's call on our lives grows out of a walk of faith! Faith is perceiving what God wants us to accomplish and living our lives in accordance with those objectives. It is the foundation on which virtue, knowledge, temperance, patience, godliness, brotherly kindness, and genuine love are established.

Rachel was busy doing the work set before her, wisely "redeeming the time" (Ephesians 5:16).

When a Man Loves a Woman

Genesis 29:10 says that when Jacob saw Rachel, he literally saw with comprehension. It was love at first sight! The Hebrew word translated "saw" in Genesis 29:10 literally means "to see with comprehension." Of course, there are those who do not believe in love at first sight. They say you must take a second and sometimes a third look. Perhaps there is some truth in the saying, "Puppy love can lead to a dog's life." I can relate to Jacob, however, because my personal experience mirrors his.

RACHEL'S OUTWARD APPEARANCE

Genesis 29 introduces Rachel; it doesn't speak of her character. "Rachel was lovely in form, and beautiful. Jacob was in love with Rachel" (29:17–18 NIV). By declaring Jacob's love right after mentioning her appearance, the implication is Rachel's beauty was, at the least, a minimal consideration in his declaration of love. Although beauty often attracts love, it doesn't end there.

THE EYE OF THE BEHOLDER

Okay men, knowing that we are visual creatures, when a man looks at a woman, his perception is overwhelmingly influenced by the emotion he feels for the one his gaze is fixed on. A man in love *sees the woman he loves as beautiful.* Studies suggest that being objectively attractive is less important to a woman's well-being than *feeling* attractive and being *treated* as attractive by a loving beholder.[1]

However, men, we can't forget that women need to be loved in ways that make them *feel* beautiful! The curious/serious gazer can uncover beauty. He doesn't dream of conquest but of discovery. He is like an explorer. He isn't interested in possessing his woman or exploiting her resources. Instead he wants to learn of her and delight in her.

It was with a curious gaze of delight that Adam first beheld Eve. She was unique, unlike any of the other creatures in his world. She moved him to wonder. Women long to be looked at the way Adam looked at Eve and Jacob gazed at Rachel: with enraptured pleasure.

If beauty is in the eye of the beholder, then a loving beholder must have the power to bring out the beauty in his beloved. In the movie *The Cooler*, starring Alec Baldwin, the cooler told his girl-friend—who had been disfigured on her face—not to judge her beauty by looking in the mirror but by looking into his eyes. Then she would truly know how beautiful she was. A husband's words of affirmation and praise have the power to turn his wife into a Rachel![2]

JACOB LOVED RACHEL UNCONDITIONALLY

The first time he laid eyes on her, Jacob knew Rachel was the woman he wanted to be his wife. His motivation for wanting to marry Rachel was *his love for her*. Genesis 29:18 says, "Jacob loved Rachel," Genesis 29:20 says Jacob loved Rachel, and Genesis 29:30

When a Man Loves a Woman

says Jacob loved Rachel. The word used to describe Jacob's love for Rachel is *hesed* in the Old Testament and is equivalent to the New Testament word *agape*.

Five words are translated "love" in the New Testament. God makes these distinctions to precisely communicate feeling, purpose, and meaning.

Phileo (friendship)—To cherish and have a tender affection for the beloved. It anticipates a response. Comradeship. Sharing. Communication. Friendship. *Phileo* is shared by dear friends who enjoy closeness and companionship. A marriage without *phileo* will be lacking, even if there is passion, since *phileo* flavors the marriage with common interests, goals, and objectives.

Storge (family love)—A natural affection and a sense of belonging to each other that is shared and expressed among parents, children, brothers, and sisters. *Storge* provides an atmosphere of security in which other forms of married love can flourish.

Epitumia (physical love)—Although not translated "love," *epitumia* is a critical aspect of married love. It denotes a strong physical desire. While not the most important aspect, it can be an indicator of the health of a marriage.

Eros (romantic love)—It includes the idea of yearning to unite with and please the loved one. Romantic, passionate, and sentimental. The kind of love poets write about in songs and poems. Exquisite pleasure. Strong. Sweet and sometimes terrifying. *Eros* is wholly emotional and cannot be summoned at will. It cannot be independent and will die if not combined with the other types of love to rejuvenate and strengthen it. *Eros* transforms a mere existence into a glorious adventure.

Finally, there is *agape.* The totally unselfish love that has the capacity to give and keep giving without expectation of anything being given in return. *Agape* values and serves in contrast to *phileo*, which cherishes and enjoys. *Agape* is the love that you can bring to marriage immediately, since it is extended as a choice of your will independent of emotion. *Agape* love is supernatural and goes on operating when every other kind of love is lacking.

The following chart may prove beneficial in comprehending my practical interpretation of how these words might express themselves in marriage.[3]

Phileo	Social	Friendship (affection)	"because of"
Stergeo	Spousal	Family love	"because of each other"
Agape	Spiritual	Faithful love	"in spite of each other"
Eros	Sensual	Fleshly	"if"

When a Man Loves a Woman

AGAPE LOVE

The love Jacob had for Rachel was genuine *agape*. It wasn't an "if you love me" or "because you love me" kind of love, but it was an unconditional and "in spite of" kind of love, the highest kind of love anyone can demonstrate. When a man *really* loves a woman, he does not love her for how she looks, what she can do for him, how she makes him feel, or even because she loves him with the same measure he loves her. This superior love is given without regard to individual achievement and superior qualities. This Jacob-style of love is not a reward for these. Looks, ability to help, and feelings are not the reason agape is given. Jacob loved Rachel for the sake of loving her. He delighted in his love for her exclusively. When a man loves a woman, he just loves her.

Jacob's expression of love toward Rachel was not unique in his day, and it is not unique today. I agree with Edith Deen who wrote in *All the Women of the Bible*: "Jacob's words are unsurpassed in the whole of romantic love literature. In fact, Jacob's service for Rachel marks him as the most devoted lover in the Bible. His love for Rachel was not a passing fancy; it would last until the end of his life."[4]

Now, let's look at what happens as Jacob *wins*, *works* for, *waits* on, *wants*, *weds*, and *warns* Rachel. These are the objectives a man has the tenacity to accomplish when he truly loves a woman.

Think about it:

1. Proverbs 18:22 (NKJV) states, "He who finds a wife finds a good thing." When you look at your mate, do you see her as a gift from God? Do you rely on God to help you treat her with unconditional love?

2. It is said that "beauty is in the eye of the beholder." What was your motivation for choosing your mate? Beyond physical appearance, name some of your mate's characteristics that initially attracted you to her. As you reflect on them, allow those qualities to be a constant reminder of your love and dedication to your mate.

3. Do you believe you can allow yourself to be vulnerable enough to love your mate the way Jacob loved Rachel?

4. In your daily prayers, ask God to show you ways to strengthen your marriage relationship.

Live by it . . .

Dear Lord,

Thank You for the privilege to come to You in prayer. I look to You for wisdom and guidance in all things. I offer You thanksgiving for the woman whom You have given me. Help me to grow in faith and in my desire to love my mate unconditionally so that she will truly become the woman You have created her to be. Amen.

When a Man Loves a Woman

Chapter Two
when a
man
loves
a woman

he affirms her identity

And it came to pass, when Jacob saw Rachel the daughter of Laban his mother's brother, and the sheep of Laban his mother's brother, that Jacob went near and rolled the stone from the well's mouth, and watered the flock of Laban his mother's brother. —Genesis 29:10

AN OLD JEWISH proverb paints a good picture of God's ordained plan that a woman's identity is distinct from a man's: "The woman was not taken from the man's head to be over him, nor from his feet to be walked on by him, but from his side to be his closest companion, from under his arm to be protected by him, near his heart to be loved by him."

God confirms this wise saying in Genesis 2:18 (NIV): "I will make a helper suitable for him." When Adam saw his gift, Eve, he said, "This is now bone of my bones and flesh of my flesh; she shall be called Woman" (Genesis 2:23). Why didn't Adam call her his wife? He would have been correct; she was his wife. Why woman? Because woman is who she is and wife is a role that she has. She is a woman before she ever becomes a wife, but she will never stop being a woman. The man who interacts with his spouse as a wife without affirming her as a woman is short-changing the relationship and setting himself up for future trouble. I believe that God affirmed more than just a woman's femininity when He created Eve. God is establishing a principle for all women, not just wives.

Adam is affirming her identity, distinct from his. Eve is a woman whether she is a wife or not. Like all women, Eve needs her femininity affirmed. God tells us in Genesis 3:6 that women have unique tastes and preferences: "The woman saw that the tree was good for food, and that it was pleasant to the eyes." As a bone, Eve was begotten from Adam. God affirmed her identity—she was a suitable helper. As a body, Eve was built for him. God affirmed her femininity. She was shaped to conform to him. As a bride, she was brought to him. God affirms her authority. She was with God and didn't even know Adam existed. God brought Eve to Adam. As a blessing, she was bestowed upon him—God affirmed her dignity. One person summarized these thoughts in one terse humorous saying, "treat her like a thoroughbred and she won't act like a nag."

THE FEMININE HEART

In *Wild at Heart: Discovering the Secret of a Man's Soul*, John Eldredge states it this way:

There are . . . three desires that I have found essential to a woman's heart, which are not entirely different from a man's and yet they remain distinctly feminine. Not every woman wants a battle to fight, but every woman yearns to be fought for. Listen to the longing of a woman's heart: She wants to be pursued. "I just want to be a priority to someone," a friend in her thirties told me.

And her childhood dreams of a knight in shining armor coming to rescue her are not girlish fantasies; they are the core of the feminine heart and the life she knows she was made for. Every woman also wants an adventure to share. Men, a lot of us make the mistake of thinking that the woman is the adventure. What we miss is that she wants to be caught up in something greater than herself.

Finally, every woman wants to have her beauty unveiled. Not to conjure, but to unveil. There is also a deep desire to simply and truly be the beauty, and be delighted in. Most little girls will remember playing dress up, or wedding day, or twirling in skirts— those flowing dresses that were perfect for spinning around in. She'll put her pretty dress on, come into the living room and twirl. What she longs for is to capture her daddy's delight. My wife remembers standing on top of the coffee table as a girl of five or six, and singing her heart out. Do you see me? Asks the heart of every girl. And are you captivated by what you see?

The world kills a woman's heart when it tells her to be tough, efficient and independent. . . . All we've offered the feminine soul is pressure to be a "good servant." No one is fighting for her heart; there is no grand adventure to be swept up in; and every woman doubts very much that she has any beauty to unveil.[5]

DELIGHT IN HER BEAUTY

First, a man can make a woman feel special by delighting in her beauty. As I stated earlier, beauty is the outward expression of the inward reality! There are some women who are obviously stunning, but even they exude an additional "shine" when looked upon and made beautiful by "the face of love"—her man's loving face that sees the woman as beautiful because he loves her. Remember, if beauty is in the eye of the beholder, then the loved woman radiates the beauty of security, and so her face can be called the "face of love."[6] We give back to the world a reflection of the love we have received. The face of love, then, is the face of one who is loved.

GIVE GIFTS THAT COMMUNICATE HIGH VALUE

To value something is to attach great importance to it. God gave me a great idea to help me affirm my wife's identity and communicate to her what a priceless treasure she is to me. I have been doing it at least once a year for the past nine years. I'll never forget the first time I blessed Leslie with one of her special days. I called one of her best friends, Maria, and told her to invite my wife out shopping. It was an invitation I knew my wife could not refuse. I even offered to pay for the entire shopping spree, gave her $50, and sent her on her way! While she was out, I cleaned the house from top to bottom and sprayed Leslie's favorite cologne throughout the house. I asked Maria to give me a call prior to bringing my wife home. I warned her not to accompany my wife to the door, because if she did, she would see her pastor as she'd never seen him before!

Leslie's eyes were wide with surprise when she stepped through the door and was greeted with, "Madam, your servant awaits your every command," as I bowed. In Hebrew, to "bow the knee" is the root meaning of *blessing*. Bowing before someone is a graphic picture of valuing that person. Leslie squealed with glee when she saw a dozen roses in the living room, a dozen in the dining room, and a dozen in the kitchen. Of course, the bow tie around my neck, towel over my arm, and silk boxers didn't hurt!

I relieved her of her bags . . . and clothing. I placed a robe around her as I led her to the bathroom, where there were another dozen roses. The aroma of peach bubble bath (her favorite) drifted through the bathroom.

I helped her into the tub and began to bathe her. As I gingerly washed her, I began to tell her how much I appreciated her and the sacrifices she had made throughout our married life. I reminded her how she gave up her home in Pittsburgh to accompany me to Chicago to train for ministry. I thanked her for giving up her educational goals in order for me to attain my degrees. I reminded her how she gave up her job and good career to stay at home so that our teenage boys would have a parent at home after school. I looked lovingly into her tear-filled eyes and began to weep as well. Our silence was deafening. It was a moment neither of us will ever forget. It is indelibly etched in our minds. I dried her off, and we put on robes and headed for our bedroom, where we dined on stuffed Cornish hens, cheese broccoli rolls made from scratch, and baked Alaska for dessert. What happened next is none of your business!

Talk to Her

The two primary elements of the special day I gave Leslie were spoken words and meaningful touch.[7]

For many Christians, words of love and acceptance are seldom heard. It is a tragedy that we withhold kindness from each other in the body of Christ, in our friendships, and in our homes. For some there is a common misconception that "just being there" communicates acceptance and blessing. Not true! More often than not, silence communicates a cavalier attitude and confusion. This is especially true for children. When they are left to fill in the blanks for themselves, they frequently arrive at the wrong conclusion.

When a Man Loves a Woman

Sadly, they do not lack for negative verbal messages that their peers are quick to impart.

Abraham blessed Isaac. Isaac blessed Jacob. Jacob gave a verbal blessing to each of his twelve sons and to two of his grandchildren. God has blessed us with the gift of His Word. He has always been a God of the spoken word. When Jesus was baptized, God spoke audibly, confirming His great pleasure with the Son: "And lo a voice from heaven, saying, This is my beloved Son, in whom I am well pleased" (Matthew 3:17). We must speak blessings. Good words are necessary to assure our loved ones of our genuine, unconditional acceptance.

Touch Her

Touch is a vital element in being a blessing to your wife. In Old Testament homes, it was always given in concert with spoken words. Kissing, hugging, and laying on of hands were all included in giving affirmation and blessing. The act of touch is significant in communicating warmth, personal acceptance—even physical health.

Over one-third of our five million touch receptors are centered in our hands![8] Interestingly, laying on of hands has become a curiosity to the medical community. Dr. Dolores Krieger, professor of nursing at New York University, has done copious research on the effects of laying on of hands. Dr. Krieger discovered that the toucher and the one being touched receive physiological benefits. This is possible because the hemoglobin that carries oxygen to the tissues is invigorated, receiving more oxygen. This increase in oxygen energizes a person and can even aid in the regenerative process if they are sick.[9]

In fact, I believe that one of the best nonverbal ways to communicate love is to hug her, because of what it can convey. It can say to a woman:

- I like touching you
- You are still desirable to me
- You are important to me
- I want to be close to you
- I am proud of you
- I want to protect you
- I care about you
- I love you

Often I conduct marriage seminars and talk about intimacy. I tell husbands that intimacy does not equal sex. It could lead to it and often sex may be a part of it. But you can be intimate without sex. To make my point I will ask the ladies to finish the sentence I start. "I don't always want to have sex, sometimes I just want you to . . ." And almost every time, every woman hollers out "HOLD ME."

When a Man Loves a Woman

Further studies confirm that meaningful touch can increase immunity, lower blood pressure, and even add up to two years to your life. A study conducted at UCLA found that just to maintain emotional and physical health, men and women need eight to ten meaningful touches each day![10] Meaningful touch is a profound way to impart blessing.

Think about it . . .

1. What is at the core of a woman's heart and why is it important for you and your mate that you find out?
2. Does your wife know that she is special to you? How do you show her?
3. In what ways do you affirm your mate's unique identity?
4. If you know that physical touch and verbal communication is integral to a woman's well-being, have you committed to affirming your mate's identity by utilizing the methods discussed in this chapter?

Live by it . . .

Dear Lord,
I am thankful that Your Word offers instruction that enables me to value my mate, first as a woman and also as my wife.

It is my heart's desire to understand the true meaning of intimacy in ways that will strengthen our relationship. Show me how to build her up so that she can live a life that is pleasing in Your sight. Amen.

When a Man Loves a Woman

Chapter Three

when a
man
loves
a woman he shows his
appreciation

JACOB REALLY cared for Rachel! Genesis 29:10 states, "And it came to pass, when Jacob saw Rachel the daughter of Laban his mother's brother . . . that Jacob *went near*, and rolled the stone from the well's mouth, and watered the flock of Laban his mother's brother" (italics mine).

The words *went near* are actually one word in Hebrew. Moses used the word in Exodus 19:15 in the present perfect tense: "And he said unto the people, Be ready against the third day: *come* not at your wives" (italics mine). The word is *nagash*, and it carries an emotional connotation. Moses uses it to instruct the Israelites to avoid romantic intimacy with their wives as part of their preparation to receive the Law of God.

REMOVING HINDRANCES TO HER SUCCESS

In regard to Rachel, *nagash* denotes the intensity of Jacob's loving concern that Rachel be able to accomplish the task before her. Jacob demonstrated that he cared about Rachel's ability to accomplish the work delegated to her by moving the stone from the mouth of the well so she could water her father's flock. His actions said, "As a woman, you should not have to move the stone, nor should you be hindered by it, Rachel. Please allow me to help you so that you can complete your work and fulfill the purpose your father has given you to accomplish today."

Help the Woman in Your Life Discover Her Purpose

In Genesis 2:23 Adam named Eve woman. Literally in Hebrew it means "from man she was taken."[11] So in essence he is identifying her by that which best corresponds to who he is. In Genesis 3 he names her Eve, mother of all living. Now it seems he is identifying her by her unique God-given purpose. You have a purpose God has given to you that I cannot fulfill and I want to give you the appropriate designation that demonstrates my awareness and appreciation of it. I heard Tony Evans once say the man who wants his wife to be exactly like him doesn't understand that if both of them are the same one of them is unnecessary.[12] That's why I call Joseph in the New Testament "Mr. Mary." His schedule eventually revolved around God's call on Mary's life to give birth to Jesus, the Messiah. He was committed to seeing the Lord's will fulfilled in Mary's life.

The greatest way to destroy a woman is to distract her from her true purpose. Conversely, the best way to encourage your woman's success is to help her discover her life's purpose. It is the desire of God's heart that each person He has given life to would accomplish the purpose that He created them for. "The plans of the Lord stand firm forever, the purposes of his heart through all generations" (Psalm 33:11 NIV).

God has purposes that He has ordained will be carried out by humanity in general, as well as purposes for men, purposes for women, and purposes for children. God has specific tasks for men to perform and women to accomplish, work that is uniquely designed for each individual. We are not the result of some divine experiment. In fact, discovering God's purpose for our lives is the key to personal satisfaction and fulfillment. When a man loves a woman, he will be committed to helping her discover the life purpose that God has placed in her heart and mind.

THE WOMAN'S PURPOSE REVEALED

Receive Love. The primary purpose of the woman was to receive love from the man, just as God's major purpose for creating man was to receive love from God. God and man maintained their spiritual relationship, but God wanted man to have someone whom he could share soul-love with. Adam had a void of intimacy. He needed to share life with humanity socially, spiritually, emotionally, and physically. "It is not good for the man to be alone. I will make a helper suitable for him" (Genesis 2:18 NIV). A woman's body reflects her role as receiver. Her ability to receive complements the man's role to give.

Perfect Match

Helpmeet as used in Genesis 2:18 (KJV) actually means that the woman was a perfect match for the man. It conveys at least two concepts: (1) someone who completes; (2) someone who complements. God took flesh from Adam and now he's half the man he used to be. He forms Eve and brings her back to Adam and now he's got back what was taken from him and more! (And it's the "more" we probably have trouble dealing with. Just joking!)

As stated earlier, men and women need each other to fulfill our mutual purposes and for balance, whether married or single!

The vitality that comes from the contribution of women should not be ignored. Women frequently have an alertness or caution in their spirit. This is frequently referred to as "intuition." There are many examples of this in Scripture.

The wife of a prosperous landowner in Shunem precisely dis-

When a Man Loves a Woman

cerned Elisha's godly character and urged her husband to assist him (2 Kings 4:8–10). The wife of a governing ruler in Jerusalem discerned the innocent character of Jesus and warned her husband not to proceed with rendering a judgment against Him (Matthew 27:19).

Have Faith. Faith is not "a shot in the dark." Rather, it is discerning what God's intended purpose is and accomplishing that purpose. More often than not, God reveals His purpose gradually in direct correspondence to how well we obey.

I liken the exercising of faith to following a narrowly lit path. Obviously, we'd all love to have one of those huge searchlights that police use to illuminate an entire neighborhood from a helicopter. But, experience has taught me, however, that God usually gives me the amount of light that I can expect to have from a flashlight, just enough for the step in front of me. I get light for the next step as I take the one preceding in obedience! Faith is a dynamic enablement that gives an individual the desire and power to accomplish God's will.

Create

Creativity is the ability to see a need, task, or idea from a unique perspective, and then meet it. Incumbent in this is honing in on the natural gifts and abilities God has bestowed on each individual. When a man loves a woman, he observes and appreciates her gifts and encourages her in them. Where is she going? What is she supposed to do? Remember, as I mentioned in chapter 2, the feminine heart wants to be a part of something larger than herself. A woman is looking to be fulfilled by committing her creativity to accomplishing a greater good.

THE KISS
"And Jacob kissed Rachel . . ." (Genesis 29:11)

The way Jacob kissed Rachel was very significant. In their culture, the way a person was kissed conveyed a specific message. If you kissed someone on the cheek, it was a kiss of cordiality. It was a standard greeting and an acceptable way to say hello. A kiss symbolized friendship and fellowship. This custom was encouraged by the apostles Paul and Peter in the New Testament with the admonition, "Greet one another with a holy kiss" (Romans 16:16 NIV).

Kissing on the lips was always a sign of affection. This possibly could have been going on in Genesis 26:8 when Abimelech realized Rebekah was Isaac's wife and not his sister. The Bible says, "It came to pass, when he had been there a long time, that Abimelech king of the Philistines looked out at a window, and saw, and, behold, Isaac was sporting with Rebekah his wife."

Kissing someone's feet was a demonstration of submission, an inferior to a superior, as in the case of subjects to kings. In fact, a king who won a war would have his feet kissed by the defeated king. The victor would then place his feet on the head of the defeated king.

It was typical for a blessing to be bestowed with a kiss on the forehead, and a kiss on the hand was a sign of approbation. The text doesn't indicate what he kissed so I don't know whether it was a kiss on the cheek, a kiss on the head, a kiss on the face, or a kiss on the forehead. But this much I do know, that all of them have an element of affection. Every man who loves a woman will need to give her at least four things: (1) acknowledgment, (2) affection, (3) attention, (4) approbation. I think it's quite easy to imply that the kiss included the first three. What may be lacking is the approbation. I think that based on the fact that Rachel is watering her father's sheep is something that should be acknowledged and appreciated.

In those days men didn't have much respect or admiration for women. Jewish men frequently prayed thanking God that they were not born women.

There was much to admire early in the relationship. Admiration should be expressed for Rachel's willingness to do what a man was supposed to do without murmuring or complaining about the work. Earlier her soon-to-be mother-in-law, Rebekah, had demonstrated the same kind of commitment. When Abraham's servant was sent to find a bride for Isaac, he would identify her by her willingness to water his camels. He had ten camels, and of course, scholars aren't agreed, but the average camel can drink about two to three gallons of water in one sitting. She watered them all.

In contemporary terms a man may express to a single mother, "I admire you! You have been abandoned and left with three children to raise all by yourself. Yet, you raised them, put them through college, and they have grown up to become respectable, contributing members of society. Please, let me do something men don't usually do. Please let me commend you, because I appreciate and admire your diligence." We need to affirm a woman's activity.

Listen, married men. Does she know how much you admire her vocation? Her appearance? Her contributions to your success? If she wears her hair to one side, you ought to notice and tell her how wonderful she looks. "I notice everything about you. You got your eyebrows arched too, didn't you? Looks good on you, girl! Kinda sexy." Then when she starts walking away: "Girl, you walkin'. You walkin', girl. Lord, have mercy, Jesus! I give in! I give up! I surrender ALL! Lookin' good, girl! You GO!"

She needs that kind of admiration, and not just in regard to her physical appearance. A woman needs spiritual, social, and intellectual affirmation. She needs to know that you care about her and appreciate her as a person. The woman in Proverbs 31 is special, isn't she? Well, she still exists today. God doesn't put a model before you that does not exist. If you believe that your woman has a ways to go to live up to the standard, then speak what you want to see into existence! Remember, "Death and life are in the power of the tongue: and they that love it shall eat the fruit thereof" (Proverbs 18:21).

Proverbs 31:28 tells us that the children of the virtuous woman rise up and call her blessed. Let me tell you what her kids do. Her kids get up in the morning and say, "Ooh, Mama! You have breakfast on the table again. Thank you. Ooh, Mama, you have lunch for us today. Thank you! Thank you for putting money in our pockets and taking us to school and to our friends' homes. We are so glad we can bring our friends to a clean house. A lot of my friends come to school dirty. I have clean clothes. Sometimes my friends don't have food. I always do. Sometimes they go home and are all alone. They have no one to talk to or to help them with their homework, but I do! Thank you, Mama." That is what her children say!

Proverbs 31:28 continues to say that the husband of the virtuous woman praises her. Here's what motivated her, what kept her going: the praise and encouragement of her husband. Her husband said, "You go, girl! Look at you. A regular little bid-nez woman. Doin' your bid-nez on the side. Doin' your thang in the house. Got your bid-nez, takin' care of the kids, keepin' the house clean . . . You got it goin' on! Oh, girl, I knew I had somethin' special when I got you . . ."

All of a sudden she feels the anointing to cook a good meal. All of a sudden she feels led by the Spirit to do the ironing. She gets gumption for dishwashing. Why? You praised her! Husbands, try to lift up your wives and tell them what you like about them, and I guarantee it will start turning—you will begin to see the things you desire to see. You will wonder what in the world is happening. You are letting her know that she is important to you. You are affirming her activity.

In fact, the statement in Proverbs 31:28 about her children rising up and calling her blessed also says that her husband praises her. Both statements are present tense. "Rise up" and "praise" are also the tense of continuous action. In other words, this was not a rare statement made after consuming an exquisite Thanksgiving meal. No! This was an ongoing, regular occurrence. Her children and husband established a regular habit of telling their mother and wife how much they appreciated her.

AN ATTITUDE OF GRATITUDE

When was the last time you sat down and took your fiancée's or wife's hand, looked her in the eyes, lowered your voice two octaves, and told her what you appreciate about her?

Jacob's sensitivity to and comprehension of Rachel's vocation seems to be intuitive. That ought not discourage any man, because we can grow in our appreciation just like Adam did for Eve.

In Genesis 2:23 Adam named Eve "woman" to show she was taken from him and intimately related to him. So he identified her by that which best represented him. In Genesis 3:20, he calls her "Eve," which means "mother of all living ones." Adam finally grows to appreciate Eve's distinctiveness apart from who he was. He recognized and acknowledged her uniqueness. Eve's distinctive design is a designation that celebrates how uniquely God created her.

Gratefulness Defined

Gratefulness means "letting others know by my words and actions how they have benefited my life." Etymologically, the central meaning of the word "gratefulness" is "to be pleased and make it known."

Three Aspects of Gratefulness

Adam learned it as a married man. Jacob exhibited it as a single man and was a good husband for Rachel, because what he needed in marriage he practiced before marriage. He knew how to appreciate a woman so he would have no problem appreciating a wife. After all, Rachel was a woman before she became a wife!

1. Realization

We must be aware of the benefits we have received! Our natural tendency is to be constantly aware of the benefits we extend and take those extended to us for granted. The first significant aspect of gratefulness is to maintain an awareness of the daily benefits we derive, versus being acutely alert only after experiencing a loss.

2. Response
After we identify how we have been blessed, our realization requires a response. I shared in a previous chapter about the value of blessings and how to give them. Also, I gave details about an annual special day I set aside to honor Leslie.

3. Responsibility
The most significant way to communicate gratitude to a benefactor is through our stewardship and generosity. "He who refreshes others will himself be refreshed" (Proverbs 11:25 NIV). The way we utilize the gifts given to us demonstrates the degree of our gratefulness.

The pioneer in discovering the impact of emotions on health, Dr. Hans Selye, concluded that vengeance and bitterness are the emotions most likely to elicit high stress levels in the human body, while gratitude is the single response most nourishing to good health.

Gratitude challenges us to keep our personal demands to a minimum and simplify our expectations of each other. Good character does not require that we allow our personal autonomy to be

When a Man Loves a Woman

trampled underfoot. Wisdom and discernment help us moderate expectations and self-seeking behavior, but not at the expense of personal care and safety.

When a man loves a woman, he cultivates the vision and purpose for his life, so that he can help cultivate and refine the life purpose of his beloved. This will be accomplished through giving her love; accepting her help, insight, and advice; and expressing gratefulness for these. He will encourage her to grow in faith and to maximize her natural gifts and abilities.

Think about it . . .

1. When it comes to your mate's ability to fulfill her God-given purpose, do you serve as a facilitator or a distracter?
2. How should a man build up his woman so she can accomplish her goals in life?
3. Does your woman know that you admire her? Explain how.
4. Are you satisfied that you are doing your best for her and your family? If not, in what ways can you improve?

Live by it . . .

Dear Lord,

I need Your help in understanding my duties as a husband. Teach me how to show unending appreciation for my mate. Please lead me and guide me in my efforts to support the love of my life so that she can discover her true purpose. Amen.

Chapter Four

when a
man
loves
a woman · he provides
security for her

WHEN A MAN loves a woman, he demonstrates his concern by making sure that she feels a sense of security. A man in love wants to make sure his woman has everything she needs to succeed and not struggle with anxiety.

LOVING CONCERN ANTICIPATES NEEDS

I believe that the character a man needs in order to be a good husband should be evident before he becomes a husband. Jacob anticipated and was willing to meet Rachel's need for assistance with moving the stone blocking the entrance to the well, so it's likely he would demonstrate the same kind of care and anticipation for her as his wife.

As a single man, Jacob implemented a New Testament concept. First Timothy 5:8 (NKJV) states, "If anyone does not provide for his own, and especially for those of his household, he has denied the faith and is worse than an unbeliever."

Paul tells Timothy that a man should anticipate the needs of his family. If he is not anticipating the needs of his wife, a husband is not adequately caring for her. If a husband does not seek to meet her spiritual, emotional, social, and material needs, then his wife may second-guess her ability to please him, and she may experience an identity crisis. A woman may question her inherent value and begin to wonder, *Am I woman enough for him?*

The Old Testament equivalent is in Genesis 22:14, where God revealed Himself to Abraham as Jehovah-Jireh. Basically, *Jireh* means "to provide." God knew that Abraham would need a lamb for a sacrifice, so God put *what* Abraham needed, *where* Abraham needed it, *when* he needed it!

When Abraham lifted up his arm to slay his only, long-awaited son in obedience, God stopped him from sacrificing Isaac, and immediately Abraham saw that God had anticipated his need. Abraham called God Jehovah-Jireh—"the God who sees before." God sees what you need before you realize you need it. Then He places what you need, where you need it, and opens your eyes to it when you need it!

Abraham saw the provision of God—a ram caught by his horns in a nearby thicket. This is a profound statement, because Abraham didn't just see a sacrificial animal that would take Isaac's place. He saw how God would provide propitiation for our sins at Calvary! God gave Abraham a glimpse into the future of humanity and allowed him to see the ultimate sacrifice who would take away the sin of the world in the person of Jesus Christ. John 8:56 says, "Your father Abraham rejoiced to see my day: *and he saw it*, and was glad" (italics added).

IMPOTENT MEN

There is a stark contrast between Jacob's attitude toward Rachel and the attitudes of the other men present at the well. The other men were so lazy, they refused to move the stone to water their own sheep. Certainly, they would not exert any effort to move the stone for Rachel. In fact, the Scriptures indicate that this was their common practice. Even though it was past time to water the flocks, the other men were waiting for someone else to move the stone for them! "And he [Jacob] said, Lo, it is yet high day, neither is it time that the cattle should be gathered together: water ye the sheep, and go and feed them. And they said, We cannot, until all the flocks be gathered together, and till they roll the stone from the well's mouth; then we water the sheep" (Genesis 29:7–8 italics mine).

The cattle should have been grazing, but they had not been watered, because the men wanted someone else to do it for them. Jacob does by himself what the other men refused to attempt to accomplish together as a group.

This type of neglect is a subtle form of hostility. It is hostile for us to presume that we are not responsible to each other or for each other! The lack of concern within the body of Christ for those who are in need is not unlike the attitude Cain had when God inquired of him, "Where is Abel thy brother?" Cain responded, "Am I my brother's keeper?" God spends the balance of Scripture addressing that issue with a persistent, unequivocal, and resounding YES.

Unfortunately, the "let someone else do it" mind-set is still prevalent today. Because the body of Christ has assumed the position that someone else will do it, there are tremendous needs that go unmet within the body of Christ! Scores of single mothers and children are living without basic needs being met; ex-prisoners are hindered from rehabilitation, for example, because we are waiting for someone else to do what each of us, as members of the body of Christ, has a mandate to do! Rather than camping on the insistence that we can't, the body of Christ, most especially men, need to insist, "If not me, then who? If not today, then when?"

FROM "DAMSEL IN DISTRESS" TO "NEW-MILLENNIUM WOMAN"

The custom of the day was that the men watered their flocks and herds first, then the women watered their flocks. Jacob moved the stone and told Rachel to come water her father's flock. If Rachel were a woman of the new millennium, she might have refused Jacob's offer.

Surprisingly enough, there are women who feel demeaned when a man offers his seat to her or opens a car door and ushers her in first. These new-millennium women don't understand that to deny this kind of attention is to relinquish some of their femininity and diminish a man's masculinity. Ironically, Christian women frequently complain that their men will not assume leadership, yet they do subtle things to emasculate and feminize them!

Society has spent the last few decades redefining what it is to be masculine. Now masculinity is more safe and feminine. Yet, women consistently ask, "Where are all the *real* men?" We asked them to be women! Every man wants to play the hero and know that he is powerful.[13] Chivalry should be welcomed by women and encouraged, particularly if they want their men to be strong, assertive leaders.

Rachel readily received Jacob's gesture of care. She acknowledged that she needed help, and I'm sure she realized that a group of women couldn't assist her with this particular task, since there was a group of men present who found it daunting for their physical capabilities.

God wants us to be interdependent! That's why we are a body. For a woman to presume that she doesn't need a man, or vice versa, is the ultimate presumption! Further, our lives are out of balance if we don't have input from men and women. Jacob was able to help Rachel because he was sensitive to Rachel's need. Rachel was happy to receive his help, and I am sure that Jacob's behavior at the well distinguished him. Since Jacob was sensitive as a single man, it is conceivable that he would be sensitive as a married man and make a good husband.

When a Man Loves a Woman, He'll Give 100 Percent

Jacob was not a fifty-fifty kind of man, like some men who say, "She's got to meet me halfway." If a relationship is a fifty-fifty proposition, where do you draw the line? In other words, how do you know when you have fulfilled your 50 percent?

As a married man, I must admit that sometimes we say some pretty stupid things, like, "You pay this bill and I will pay another . . ." No! In the spirit of establishing a spirit of oneness, why don't we pool our resources and pay our bills together because we are one?

We can learn from Jacob that the man is the initiator in a love relationship, and the woman is the responder. As the thermostat, the man generally sets the climate for the relationship, and the woman usually registers it. Her very body, as discussed in the previous chapter, illustrates her posture to receive.

Rachel can be secure because she knows her needs will be anticipated and met. She is confident that she will get the attention that she desires and deserves, because when a man loves a woman, he will make her feel secure.

Think about it . . .

1. As Christians, prayer time is an important element of our lives. On a regular basis, do you talk to the Lord about fulfilling your responsibility to be the provider of your home?

2. Are you spending adequate time in prayer so that God can help you to anticipate your mate's needs?

3. In what ways do you take action and provide a secure environment that will contribute to your mate's success? Explain.

4. If you haven't already done so, set aside a part of your day to spend quality time with God. The benefits of doing so are endless.

Live by it . . .

Dear Lord,

In recognition of the importance of prayer, I ask that You help me to be a man who relies on daily communication with You. Show me how to remove any anxiety that my mate may have over her need to feel secure. I want to replace her struggles with confidence in my ability and willingness to provide for her. Amen.

When a Man Loves a Woman

Chapter Five

when a
man
loves
a woman

he expresses his affection

And Jacob kissed Rachel, and lifted up his voice, and wept.
—Genesis 29:11

I love you, not only for what you are,
but for what I am when I am with you.
I love you, not only for what you have made of yourself,
but for what you are making of me.
I love you for the part of me that you bring out.
I love you for putting your hand into my heaped-up heart
and passing over all the foolish, weak things that you can't
help dimly seeing there,
and for drawing out into the light all the beautiful belongings
that no one else had looked quite far enough to find.

I love you because you are helping me to make of
the lumber of my life not a tavern, but a temple,
out of the works of my every day not a reproach but a song.[14]

WHEN A MAN LOVES A WOMAN, HE WINS HER WITH COMPASSION

Notice verse 11 says Jacob "lifted up his voice, and wept." Jacob wins Rachel with compassion. He lifted up his voice and wept. This wasn't a silent sob. It was a soprano cry, not a bass one.

Wait a minute! This is powerful and virtually unheard of. A man who is not ashamed to cry in the open in front of a woman while other men are looking at him. When I arrived at this point in the Scripture, I cried. Why did I cry, you ask? Well, I will tell you why.

I cried because I thought of the hundreds of couples I have counseled over the years. Frequently, I see women who have been verbally or physically mistreated by a husband who just sits there stoic, cold, and uncaring. He didn't want to come for counseling in the first place and had to be coerced, literally kicking and screaming the whole way. Then, when he gets to my office, everything is her fault, and he doesn't accept any responsibility for the current problems in the relationship. I have seen women literally get down on their knees, begging their husbands to listen and consider their part, only to have the men turn a cold shoulder. So I weep for these women, because, as a pastor, it has been the hardest thing I have had to see.

To see and to hear the lack of consideration and brutal unkindness in some of these men . . . They think a woman is some kind of plaything or a toy. It's in counseling sessions with this type of man when I get very angry. I know it is the Spirit of God who stops me from getting up and clocking him.

Jacob would have never exhibited such a mean spirit to Rachel. Jacob's tears were tears of compassion and an overt demonstration of empathy and affection.

THE COMMAND "TO LOVE"

Women need affection from their husbands. A woman needs her husband to love her. There aren't any Scriptures that I am aware of that *command* a woman to love a man. Titus 2 says older women should teach the younger women *how* to love their husbands. Why does God command a man to love his wife, but doesn't command a woman to love her husband? Perhaps because women have a natural inclination to be loving. Men need to work at it!

Men often ask, "Why isn't she giving me the kind of love I want?" Perhaps because you are not invoking that privilege. I can guarantee that you are not making the right kind of investment if you are asking this question.

A woman is like a bank account. If you make a love deposit in her emotional bank account, she will accept it, allow your investment to accrue interest, and then give it back to you in greater measure than what you originally deposited.

Conversely, if you give her drama, then she will give drama back to you. That drama will be pressed down, shaken together, and running over in abundance. If you are taking a love check to her emotional bank and submitting it for cash without sufficient funds in the account, your check is going to return to you as "Insufficient Funds," because you cannot take out more than what you have deposited into the account. Yet, there are many of us trying to cash a $1000.00 check when we only have a balance of $100. Men, it doesn't work that way.

AFFECTION IS THE DEMONSTRATION OF COMPASSION

Women want affection! Dr. Willard Harley, in his book *His Needs, Her Needs*, says that affection is a woman's number one need. He calls it "the first thing she can't do without."

To most women, affection symbolizes security, protection, comfort, and approval. Affection is a vitally important commodity in the eyes of a woman. When a husband shows his wife affection, he sends these messages: I will take care of you and protect you. You are important to me.[15]

In fact, have you ever considered the power of a hug? Of course,

When a Man Loves a Woman

a hug is just a little thing, but it is a powerful demonstration of affection. A hug says, I like touching you. You are very desirable to me. You are very important to me. I want to be close to you. I am proud of you. I want to protect you. We are one. I love you. I like taking care of you. I am on your side.

In the movie *Milk Money*, three twelve-year-old boys asked leading actress Melanie Griffith if there is a place on a girl's body where you can touch her and she will go crazy. In the beginning of the movie, she tells them no such spot exists. At the end of the movie, Ms. Griffith turns to the boys and says, "Hey, boys, there is a place you can touch a woman and drive her crazy. Right here," as she points to her heart.

Jacob knew that too! He knew that when a man loves a woman, he will know how to touch her heart with displays of compassion and affection!

Think about it . . .

1. Take some time to consider this: When it comes to the issues in your marriage, do you believe everything is her fault?

2. What do you think would happen if you tried to see things from her perspective? What changes would you make in your relationship to remedy some of your problems?

3. Have you ever tried to make a withdrawal from your wife's emotional bank account only to find the response, "Insufficient Funds"?

4. In what special ways can you express affection to your wife before you attempt to withdraw from her emotional bank account?

Live by it . . .

Dear Lord,

I come to You now realizing You are the Source of all wisdom and knowledge. Teach me how to touch my mate's heart in ways that provide the kind of affection, protection, comfort, and approval that she craves. Amen.

When a Man Loves a Woman

Chapter Six

when a
man
loves
a woman

he establishes companionship

ALLOW ME TO reiterate. Everything Jacob needed to be in the marriage, he was before the marriage, even before he knew there was going to be a marriage. Jacob demonstrated these characteristics to this woman not sure that she would be his wife. He did it because he was a man of character.

WHEN A MAN LOVES A WOMAN, HE WILL WIN HER WITH CONVERSATION

In his book *Lonely Husbands, Lonely Wives*, Dennis Rainey relates the following story:

My daughter, Ashley, slipped into my study and asked me what I was writing about. "Isolation," I replied. "Do you know what that means?"

"Oh," said my blue-eyed, blonde-haired, freckle-faced ten-year-old who replies, "That's when somebody excludes you." I may be a bit prejudiced, but I like Ashley's answer better than the dictionary's definition, which says isolation is "the condition of being alone, separated, solitary, set apart."[16]

I think Ashley's definition is profoundly accurate too. When you are excluded, you have a feeling of distance. There is a lack of intimacy and closeness. What makes isolation and exclusion especially devastating, though, is the idea that there is a person or persons who intentionally, with forethought, want to make you feel alone! Not only are they not concerned about your solitude, but they want you to experience it. They are cruel and calculating in their exclusion. You may have sex, but you don't have love; you may live together, but you don't share life and common interests. You may talk, but you don't communicate.

Communication is a process of sharing information, either verbally or nonverbally with another person in such a way he or she understands what you are saying. In his excellent book *Why Am I Afraid to Tell You Who I Am?*[17] John Powell asserts that we communicate on at least five different levels, from shallow

When a Man Loves a Woman

clichés to deep personal honesty. Hang-ups such as fear, apathy, or a poor self-image keep us at the shallow level, but if we can be freed from our weaknesses, we can move to the deeper, more meaningful level. Powell's five levels of communication include:

Level Five: Cliché Conversation. This type of talk is safe. We use words such as "How are you?" "How is your family?" "Where have you been?" "I like your suit." In this type of conversation there is no personal sharing. Each person remains safely behind his screen.

Level Four: Reporting the Facts to Others. In this kind of conversation we are content to tell others what someone else has said, but we offer no personal commentary on these facts. We just report the facts like the five o'clock news each day. We share gossip and little narrations, but we do not commit ourselves as to how we feel about it.

Level Three: My Ideas and Judgments. This is where some real communication begins. The person is willing to step out of his solitary confinement and risk telling some of his ideas and decisions. He is still cautious, however, and if he senses that what he is saying is not being accepted, he will retreat.

Level Two: My Feelings or Emotions. Now the person shares how he feels about facts, ideas, and judgments. The feelings underneath these areas are revealed. If a person is to really share himself with another individual, he must get to the level of sharing his feelings.

Level One: Complete Emotional and Personal Truthful Communication. All deep relationships, especially marriage relationships, must be based on absolute openness and honesty. This may be difficult to achieve because it involves a risk—the risk of being rejected because of our honesty, but it is vital for relationships to grow in marriage. There will be times when this type of communication is achieved and other times when the communication is not as complete as it should be.

These are five suggested levels of communications. Only you know at what level communication is occurring in your marriage. But ask yourself, what is our communication like? Which level are we? How can we move toward Level One in our relationship?

ELEMENTS OF AFFIRMING COMMUNICATION

Affirming communication avoids prideful presumption. The Hebrew word for "presumption" describes a person who has an exaggerated sense of self, who assumes more authority than he has been given. A presumptuous person believes he is entitled to things that do not belong to him. He ventures into areas that go beyond recognizable limits.

Affirming communication is free from scorn. A scorner uses facial expressions to communicate disdain and contempt. He shows repugnance toward people and ideas that contradict his erroneous

When a Man Loves a Woman

conclusions. Scorn is expressed in attitudes, behavior, and speech.

Affirming communication will also avoid any message that can create disillusionment. An illusion is an erroneous perception of reality. Thus, disillusionment means to destroy one's illusions. In other words, when a man loves a woman, he will communicate in sincerity, without expectation, being careful not to make promises he can't keep or create unrealistic expectations or false perceptions. He will just be "real."

In contrast, affirming communication comes from a heart that is wise, wholesome, encouraging, contrite, pure, and upright. A wise heart listens actively and eagerly receives. A wholesome heart is curative! It is not easily overthrown or turned. A heart full of encouragement knows how to calm fears, giving strength to the faint, and visualize circumstances and situations from God's perspective. A contrite heart is conscience-led and humbled, demonstrating a decreasing estimation of himself. John the Baptist exemplifies this when he concludes, "He must increase, but I must decrease" (John 3:30). A pure heart is singular. It involves transparency. A pure heart does not have conflicting motives or a hidden agenda. Finally, an upright heart describes a person who is reliable and has integrity. David resolved, "I will behave myself wisely in a perfect way. . . . I will walk within my house with a perfect heart" (Psalm 101:2).

NONVERBAL COMMUNICATION

There are three elements of communication. Not only do we convey our thoughts with words, but rhetoricians (*those skilled in the use of language to persuade*) tell us that when you speak, 50 percent of what you communicate is declared by your tone, 30 percent by your body language, with only 20 percent of how you feel actually communicated by your words.

For example, my wife says, "Honey, will you take out the garbage?" and I say, "Yeah," in a sarcastic tone and stay on the couch watching TV. Her response is, "No. Don't take it out." Then I say, "Well, I said yeah." Next there is an explosion.

"Now why are you getting an attitude, huh? You asked me to take the garbage out. I'm getting ready to take the garbage out. Why are you getting an attitude, huh? You know I don't like the way . . ."

Wait a minute. Didn't I say yeah? I said yes, but my body language and my tone said no.

Things usually escalate from there, don't they? My wife concludes, "Okay, you don't want to take out the garbage. That's all right. I'll let you know there are plenty of men who want to take my garbage out."

Now, you know I don't like that, so I respond, "Well, you better go ahead and call one." The fight really starts when she walks toward the phone!

A loving husband understands that when a man loves a woman,

When a Man Loves a Woman

he will talk to her. He will communicate with her. Why?

Jacob realizes that intimacy is created and solidified through communication. Soul ties are formed through words. Words heal (Proverbs 12:18). They can promote understanding when the speaker forgoes a determination to be right (Proverbs 18:2). They convey acceptable things (Proverbs 10:32).

WOMEN ARE VERBAL, AND INTIMACY IS BUILT THROUGH COMMUNICATION

All you have to do is look at your phone bill to know that women are verbal creatures! Now, I know there are exceptions to the rule, but in general this is the case.

You Don't Talk to Me!

If you are having problems in your relationship because your wife says, "You don't talk to me," what is she really saying? You don't talk to her! You wonder, *Where is this coming from?* Well, it's coming from the amount of time and attention you spent talking with her prior to getting married as compared to how much you talk with her now.

Look, brothers, you have to rap, and you ought to know it by now! How did you win her? You talked. You told her how much you loved her. You commented on everything. You said this. You said that . . . You must continue to do that.

It's like the story of the man who had been married for forty years. His wife asked, "Do you love me?"

He said, "Look, honey. I told you forty years ago that I love you. If I change my mind, you'll be the first to know."

My wife can tell me once a year, "I love you." That's good enough for me. She told me last year she loved me. She said it again this year, but she really didn't need to. I speak to her every day, and every day guess what I say. "I love you, Leslie." Doesn't she know that? Of course! There are exceptions to every rule, but by and large, women appreciate affirmation because it creates a sense of security for the present. Yes, I said "I love you" yesterday, but she needs a reaffirmation of that fact today. I have to do it. You have to do it, and you must keep doing it. This is especially important during the summertime when it's hot and some women are not as modest as they should be—know what I'm sayin'? You must reaffirm your wife and reassure her that she's the only one for you. "There's no one else for me, and I want you to know that."

She thought that communication between the two of you would increase once you were living together, not decrease. You don't talk as much as you did before you won her. You've cut off communication, and you're wondering why she's like she is? Because she still desires and needs conversation with you. Follow these principles to become more effective in your communication:

1. Initiate conversation. This communicates "I like talking to you."

2. Get rid of distractions. Turn off the television to convey "You are important to me, more important than what I am currently doing."

3. Make eye contact. This shows you are receptive to what's being said.

4. Wear a pleasant expression. Your face will communicate that you are enjoying the conversation.

5. Use vocal clutter. (*Interject during the short pauses.*) This shows that you are listening and empathize.

6. Use appropriate touching. If you touch her face while she is talking, you are telling her that you love her. If you take her hand, you communicate sympathy and sensitivity to her feelings. An arm around her says, "I will protect you."

7. Give an affirmative conclusion. This is where you convey that if things are not resolved, you are open to listening whenever she feels the need to discuss the issue again.

WOMEN BELIEVE THAT QUESTIONS
ARE SYNONYMOUS WITH CARING

Women ask lots of questions. When men ask questions, it's for the purpose of gathering information or attempting to solve a problem. Women ask questions to carry on a conversation. Let me set up the scenario:

"Baby, what did you do today? What happened in your ministry?"

"Uh, nothing much."

"Well, what was the nothing you did all day?"

"Uh, I talked to this person, that person."

"Well, what happened?"

"Nothing . . . you know."

"What did you do for lunch?"

"Picked up something quick."

"Where did you go afterward?"

"Made a run."

Now, when two brothers talk, things are pretty cut-and-dried:

"Yeah, man, xyz . . ."

"That's it?"

"Yeah. End of story."

Here's what's happening. He's thinking, *Why is she asking all these questions? I'm a grown man. She's trying to check up on me.*

She wants to know too much. Why's she got to know all that?

Because she is trying to create an atmosphere of intimacy, and that is done through conversation. You have been apart for eight to ten hours, and your worlds have not merged. Now she wants to be brought into your world. The only way that can happen is if you tell her what happened in your world so that she can feel a part of it and who you are.

A woman thinks, *If I don't ask, he'll think I don't care.* That's why women ask lots of questions. I'm telling you, brothers, the number one reason women ask is because they care about you.

By and large, questions for men represent meddling. Women, on the other hand, use them to express caring. To flip the script: If you come home after work and don't ask about her day, what you have communicated by not opening your mouth is, "I don't care about what you went through today. It really doesn't matter to me. I'm not concerned. You probably didn't do anything important anyway . . . It doesn't matter because I didn't ask you."

UNDERSTANDING THE WAY YOUR PARTNER COMMUNICATES

My wife would say, "James, I need to tell you something that is very important. This is going on . . ." I would look her dead in the eye. I wouldn't look left or right. She would say, "You are not listening to me."

I would say, "Wow. Baby, I'm standing right here looking you eye to eye. What in the world? Why would you say I'm not listening and that I don't care?"

"You don't," Leslie would respond. "You're looking at me, but your mind is a thousand miles away. I can see through your empty eyes right to your brain. You're just staring off into space."

Yet, I would be paying full attention. She thinks I'm not listening because I am not interacting in a way that a woman converses. I'm not saying, "Uh-huh. Whoa! Yeah."

Let me set the scenario up again:

When two women talk, they show interest with lots of interjections:

"Yeah. What happened next, girl? . . . For reaaa-al? . . ."

"Chile' pleeez . . . Uh-huh. Know you right, girl frien . . ."

I decided that when Leslie related a story to me, I would say, "Yeah, girl. Um-hmm. Lord have mercy, Jesus!" When I first started that practice, she told me, "You better quit pickin' at me, James!" Now she continues with the story, because I continued to interject (*use vocal clutter*) and proved to her that I was expressing genuine interest in what she had to say. Today when she says, "So and so . . ." and I say, "Help me now, somebody!" Leslie doesn't take a break and proceeds with her story.

WOMEN HAVE A UNIQUE PERSPECTIVE

There is another difference in the way women communicate that is very profound, significant, and important to understand. Unfortunately, most men do not realize this difference or value how helpful these differing perspectives can be in decision making when given just regard to their proportional relevance or importance. In addition, to value each of these perspectives and be committed to attentive listening further communicates security to a woman.

The four points of view or perspective that a woman will communicate from are:

1. Intellectual
2. Emotional
3. Volitional
4. Spiritual

A response from an *intellectual* perspective will say, "That makes sense. I think it's a good idea."

Emotional will say, "I feel very uneasy about this decision. I don't feel good about this. I have a 'feeling' . . ."

A *volitional* insight will say, "I have decided to allow you to make this decision, or I have decided that you have done more research in this area than I have, or I have decided that I am right about this."

Communicating from a *spiritual* perspective may include her giving you Scripture references, interpreting a potential solution or pitfall based on biblical principles, or simply communicating, "I am sure that God is going to teach me/you/us important lessons through the resolution of this issue."

Most men become confused when women switch from one perspective to another. They don't understand that women use conversation as a catharsis, because even though there may be a point-in-time decision, women need their emotions to catch up with their will, or intellect.

That's why all of a sudden, weeks after the two of you have resolved an issue, she revisits it. You get mad because she's bringing it up. You think she's trying to put you down for past mistakes, when she really hadn't completely resolved things. Our guilt causes us to cut off further discussion. We need to let women talk it through. When we refuse to do so, we ultimately prolong the drama.

God explains that "counsel in the heart of man [woman] is like deep water; but a man of understanding will draw it out" (Proverbs 20:5). Taking the time to patiently consider and think through the four perspectives your wife communicates from ensures that you can benefit from her unique ability to consider an issue from different angles. The most important benefits are that you will bolster her feelings of security, self-worth, intelligence, value, judgment, and significance. To neglect attentive listening is to reject her God-given role as a helpmeet to you. "Likewise, ye husbands, dwell with them according to knowledge, giving honour unto the wife, as unto the weaker vessel, and as being heirs together of the grace of life; that your prayers be not hindered" (1 Peter 3:7).

Think about it . . .

1. Consider the Scripture in Proverbs 18:12. Does your communication with your mate promote understanding between the two of you? Explain.

2. Does your nonverbal communication indicate that you are less interested in what she has to say and more interested in what you are doing at a given time?

3. Does learning about the four (4) perspectives of a woman (intellectual, emotional, volitional, spiritual) help you understand more clearly how women think? Why or why not?

4. How does it make you feel when your mate brings up something you thought was resolved a week ago, a month ago, a year ago? Explain how you react.

Live by it . . .

Dear Lord,

I truly want to make my marriage stronger. Help me to rely on You through my prayerful communication with You. Help me to realize how important it is not only that I share what is on my heart, but to also listen to Your response. Teach me how to wait patiently for You to answer. Amen.

Chapter Seven

when a man loves *a woman*

he will work for her

And Jacob served seven years for Rachel; and they seemed unto him but a few days, for the love he had to her.
—Genesis 29:20

WHEN A MAN loves a woman, he demonstrates it through a commitment to his work. Through his commitment, Jacob demonstrated that he knew how to provide for a wife. "And he said, Lo, it is yet high day, neither is it time that the cattle should be gathered together: water ye the sheep, and go and feed them. And they said, We cannot, until all the flocks be gathered together, and till they roll the stone from the well's mouth; then we water the sheep" (Genesis 29:7–8).

Who is Jacob talking to? He's speaking to the brothers sitting by the mouth of the well. I believe God mentions the men in this text to highlight and contrast Jacob's determination with the lack of initiative of the men sitting around, convinced the task was too big for them. The brothers are at the well in the middle of the day. Jacob comes along and says, "Hey. What's up? Why are you lounging around, laying in the cut? Why are you standing on the corner? The sheep are here. The well is here. McDonald's is across the street. Why don't you water the sheep so they can graze? Why don't you get a job? Why don't you get off your lazy behind and do something?"

They replied, "We cannot."

"Well, why can't you?"

"Because we're waiting for somebody to move the stone and uncover the well. When the other brothers come and do that for us, then we will be able to water the sheep."

Rachel's at the well to water her father's flock, she sees this new guy, and he's taking the stone from the mouth of the well . . . alone! I can imagine her saying, "Whoa! *Who* is that? Umm, chile, let me move this veil a little lower and see who that is . . . Look at the regulars, standing around the way they do every day. They have to wait on their boys since they don't have the courage to attack a big job alone. They can't do anything alone, which means I have to wait on them so that I can have a turn at the well. Look at that! This new man moved the stone cover all by himself. I don't know who he is, but I know he's not part of the regular crowd. Kinda strong too. Now that's a *real* man!"

When Jacob asked the men why they were standing around, they used custom and protocol as an excuse. At least Jacob by his words and his actions seems to assume it's an excuse.

When Jacob asked the men why they were standing around, they gave him excuse after excuse. Similar excuses are prevalent today. "I can't find a job." Well, you certainly can't find a job if you aren't getting up to go look for one. If you look for a job long enough and hard enough, you will find one. "It's institutional racism. Black men are castrated by society." I don't deny that, but if that is the general rule and a valid reason for your unemployment, then there isn't a brother who should have a job. Others say, "Well, you know, my daddy wasn't around to show me how to be a man." He's not around now. How did you eat today? Who feeds you now, your mother? "I was mistreated as a child." What does that have to do with your ability to eat today? Assuredly, God gives all of His children the grace to overcome anything in our past. The problem is, we allow circumstances to circumvent us, and we resist the grace available to us. Granted, the economy is bad and it is much harder to find a job than it used to be. But my question to you is, "Are you even trying?"

So, the men at the well made excuses while Jacob went to work and moved the stone all by himself. Then he watered Rachel's sheep. On a normal day, Rachel had to wait until all the men were finished watering their flocks before she had an opportunity to tend to her father's sheep.

Jacob distinguished himself from all the other brothers. I can imagine them saying, "Look at him showing off." Jacob knew something they didn't. Boys playfully wait around, while men get right to work.

MOTHERS OF ADULT ADOLESCENT SONS

Contemporary mothers have created some of today's catastrophes that married women are living with. You allowed your son to remain at your breast until he was thirty-five years old! . . . and you wonder why his wife is frustrated with him.

If you have the misfortune of parenting an "adolescent adult," it's not too late to urge him to grow up! Keep hope alive. Here's what you have to do. If you get up at six o'clock in the morning to go to work while he lies in bed, don't fret. You can help him change by changing your enabling behavior. If you get up at six, he gets up at six. If you leave at seven, he leaves at seven. When he leaves at seven, you tell him, "Stay out there until you find a job." Take his keys, because if you don't, he will go back into the house once he thinks you are gone.

The future wife of your son will thank you for helping him develop the character of Jacob and instilling in him the determination to find enough work to support his family, even if that means he has to work at McDonald's, Burger King, and Wendy's all at the same time.

Don't miss what Jacob is demonstrating that the other men are not able to say: "I know how to take care of a woman, Rachel. I have a commitment to work. I will work to provide for you. When other men stand around waiting for a handout and don't know what a W-2 or a 1099 is, I will work to take care of you."

WORKING WIVES

There are working wives who will not appreciate this, but I appeal to them to pay close attention and consider the following. When you attempt to carry the financial burden of your household, you deprive your husband of the opportunity to fulfill a significant part of his God-ordained purpose. Just as it was not Rachel's responsibility to move the stone from the mouth of the well, it is not your responsibility to be the primary breadwinner for your family. You rob yourself of one of the benefits of marriage, you deny the man the privilege and obligation of working to win you, and you interfere with a significant aspect of his establishing his identity and self-worth.

You may not agree with it, but it is my opinion that if your lifestyle takes two incomes and necessitates that your wife must work, then you need to begin downsizing. Look at people who sacrificed their relationships on the altar of materialism. Ask them if all the material wealth contributed to the well-being of their relationship or ushered the breakdown of their relationship. You should downsize your living until you're able to provide for primary needs from his income alone. A couple in the church that I pastor sold their five-bedroom house and bought a three-bedroom home, cut up their credit cards as they paid them off, and made the necessary adjustment to live off of his income. They are doing very well, and she's at home helping to raise their children.

Some of you may remember living in an apartment when you didn't have two nickels to rub together, but you were happy. Now you have all the things but no time for each other, because you forgot you were supposed to love people and use things, not love things and use people. Quit using your wife as a means to get more material things and end up coming out on the short end in your relationship with her and your children.

What are you saying, Pastor Ford? I'm saying if you're in a big house and you have a lot of bill pressures, sell it. Move to a smaller house, go back to an apartment, whatever you have to do to maintain healthy relationships with your wife and children. Don't allow the materialism of the world to take away from what God has ordained to happen within the confines of marriage.

A WORKINGMAN'S SATISFACTION

Now men, you can't expect a woman to work a full-time job outside the house, then come home and do a full-time job in the house. If she's going to work forty hours outside the home, quit expecting her to do everything in the home. If you want her to share in your financial responsibility, then you need to share in chores. Start doing some of the cooking and cleaning. You cry, "I don't know how to do it." Well, she had to learn. You can learn too. Get her to teach you how to do laundry so you don't put colored clothes and white clothes together in hot water, for example.

Instead of coming home and waiting for something to be cooked for you, you do the cooking. It's easy. If you're going to have spaghetti, go to your local grocery store. You've seen them. Buy some spaghetti, probably "no. 8." When you get home, all you have to do is get a pot. Fill it with water. Turn on the stove. Place the pot on the stove and let the water boil. Put some oil (cooking oil, men. It will most likely be in the kitchen, not the garage!) in the water so that the spaghetti doesn't stick together. Place a pound of spaghetti in the water. Let it boil. Test the spaghetti with a fork. If it's real hard, it isn't ready yet. Don't let it get too soft either.

Next, get a frying pan. Put it on the stove. Turn the stove on. Put some salt in the bottom of the frying pan. Now you are going to brown the ground beef, turkey, or chicken that you purchased at the store when you bought your spaghetti. Place it in the heated skillet. How do you brown it, you wonder? Just keep turning it until it turns from red to brown. Then you get some Prego or Ragu and you pour the oil off your browned meat. Let me say it again.

Pour the oil off of the browned meat in the skillet. Take a sieve. Remove the spaghetti from the pot, pour it in the sieve, let the water run off. Combine the spaghetti, meat, and the sauce and stir. The spaghetti is finished.

Now, get a head of lettuce. Cut it up. Cut and combine tomatoes, a bell pepper, and maybe some mushrooms. Place all the salad fixings in a large bowl. Mix. Get some Italian bread. Cut it in half. Spread butter and sprinkle garlic powder on the bread. Warm it in the oven on broil until the top turns light brown. Voilá, dinner!

Within the recesses of every woman's heart, there are two voids. One of them can only be filled with Jesus Christ. The other can only be satisfied by a man, whose sole purpose is to make her the happiest woman in the world. A man's commitment to work communicates affirmation to a woman. Jacob's actions say, "You are a woman, Rachel, and you should not have to tend sheep. The other men may refuse to acknowledge it, but I realize that this is a man's job. I want to affirm your identity as a woman. Please, allow me to help you."

Now it is clear that God placed those guys who lacked initiative around the well to highlight and contrast Jacob's initiative and commitment to work. While the other guys were waiting for someone to do something, Jacob knew that when a man loves a woman, he is always willing to take the initiative to meet her needs. Always.

Think about it . . .

1. Are you out of a job? The economy has made it tough to find employment in most cases. Will you use that as an excuse not to provide for your family? Or will you work at finding a job as hard as you can?

2. If you are struggling to pay your bills and materialism has crept into your once happy home, are you willing to downsize to regain a peaceful environment within your home?

3. Think on some of the happier times in your marriage and what made those times so pleasant. List five to ten ideas and decide to recreate those moments to the best of your ability.

4. Are you willing to share the workload at home with your wife if she works outside of the home? Why or why not?

Live by it . . .

Dear Lord,

I bring my life to You now. As I commit my ways to You, I confess my failures. Lord, I admit that I can do better. I am willing to take the initiative to meet the needs of my mate and our household. Please enable me to be the kind of provider that You would have me to be. I want to take my God-ordained place and fill the void in my mate's heart. Amen.

Chapter Eight
when a
man
loves
a woman

he wants only her

Many waters cannot quench love, nor will rivers overflow it; if a man were to give all the riches of his house for love, it would be utterly despised. —Song of Solomon 8:7 NASB

WHEN A MAN loves a woman, he doesn't want anyone else. Even though Jacob was stuck in a culture where he had to take Leah as his wife, he never acted as if he loved her. Jacob never wanted Leah. In fact, when you observe how Moses summarizes the history of Jacob in Genesis 46, it seems to validate Jacob's desire for Rachel and not for Leah. When Moses mentions the children of Jacob through the handmaids Zilpah and Billah, he uses parallel thought in verses 18 and 25.

"These are the sons of Zilpah, whom Laban gave to Leah his daughter, and these she bare unto Jacob, even sixteen souls."

"These are the sons of Billah, which Laban gave unto Rachel his daughter, and she bare these unto Jacob: all the souls were seven."

He also uses a parallel structure when he tells of the children of both sisters to bare to Jacob in verses 15 and 22. But he includes one statement in the chapter about Rachel that he doesn't make about Leah. In verse 19 he says "the sons of Rachel Jacob's wife." Moses summarizes this family history, calling Rachel Jacob's wife and omitting that designation from Leah! What does it mean? You tell me, you already know what I think! He worked fourteen years for Rachel. That's who he loved. He wanted only her. Jacob was a one-woman man. No one else could fit the bill. Rachel met all his needs.

Jacob never had this problem with Rachel. He always had eyes only for her, even though he had another wife, Leah. "And he went in also unto Rachel, and he loved also Rachel more than Leah, and served with him [Laban] yet seven other years" (Genesis 29:30).

Why was Leah rejected? It is not Jacob's fault. It's Laban's fault. Leah's father pushed her on a man who never really wanted her. Jacob never loved Leah. Leah's father insisted that Jacob accept her in order to receive his true love, Rachel. That's why Leah was "dogged-out."

Let me just stick a pin right here and tell you something, men. While the marriage of Jacob and Leah was no fault of Jacob, the woman you plan to marry should be someone whom you have picked to honor and cherish for the rest of your life.

If you marry someone and decide later that you don't love her, the consequences will most likely result in one or both of you saying "I want a divorce!" because you will treat her as if you don't love her. This is a situation that you want to and can avoid. Women are to be treated with love and respect. So men, don't play with a woman's feelings. Sometimes we think we are in love and we really aren't. That's a tragic thing when a man thinks he loves a woman or when a woman thinks a man loves her and he really doesn't. If you don't love her, man-up and break it off so that she won't have to suffer any longer with someone who never intended to treat her as the beautiful person God created her to be.

Time and time again I've tried to tell the brothers to settle down with a good woman whom they love and who loves them.

For instance, I have two brothers who are not saved. When one of them comes to visit us in Chicago, he likes to visit a club called the "50 Yard Line." One night I asked him how he enjoyed his evening. He exclaimed, "Oh man! It was smokin'. I had my choice of women! That place is a player's delight!"

I reminded him that anyone can have a lot of women, but it takes a real man to go the distance with one woman and be faithfully committed to her. I commend men who are faithful to their wives, especially in the day in which we live. This morally decadent contemporary culture makes an extramarital affair easy.

Have you heard the story about the guy whose wife asked him if he would remarry if she died? He responded, "No. Oh no, of course not. No way."

She said, "Oh. You don't like being married?"

"Well, wait a minute. Yeah."

"So you wouldn't get married again?"

"Well, yeah, I guess so. Yeah. Okay. I'll get married again. After all, I do enjoy being married."

"Would you let her live in my house?"

"Well, yeah."

"You would? Would you bring her into our bedroom?"

"Yeah."

"You'd take my pictures out of the frame and put hers up?"

"Yeah."

"You would? You'd let her use my golf clubs?"

"No. She's left-handed."

That's a funny vignette, but Jacob would not tease in that way. He never considered a life without Rachel. I told Leslie that if she ever leaves me, I'm going with her! One day in the middle of a heated argument, she started packing her suitcases. "I'm leaving," she bellowed.

I grabbed my suitcase and started packing and said, "I'm leaving too! Where we going?"

No wonder Leah was jealous. She wanted what Jacob could only give to Rachel.

When a man loves a woman, he wants her and no one but her.

Jacob was an "eagle" man! The American bald eagle is a one-eagle man for a lifetime. He is totally committed to one female eagle his entire life. If his mate dies, he never hooks up with another female eagle.

God has Moses, the writer of the book of Genesis, to give glowing testimony to the commitment that Jacob has to Rachel. Genesis 46 lists all of Jacob's family who went to Egypt. Verse 15 lists the sons of Leah and verse 19 lists the sons of Rachel. Yet even though Leah was the first one married to Jacob, she was not called his wife. But verse 19 states, "the sons of Rachel Jacob's wife" (quotations mine).

What a tribute to Jacob's commitment. Rachel is the only one recognized as his woman. He's committed to her. He wants her and no one but her.

Think about it . . .

1. When you think of your woman, what are some of the things that help you remember why you married her and that she's the only one for you?
2. What will it take for you to treat your woman with the same love and admiration now that you did when you first married her?
3. It takes a strong relationship with God to maintain a strong marriage. Do you plan to honor and cherish your wife for the rest of your lives?

Live by it . . .

Dear Lord,

I submit to Your will and depend on Your power to help me remain a faithful and devoted husband. My desire is to emulate the faithfulness You show to me in ways that my mate can feel in a tangible way. As I place my faith in You, I know that You will continue to bless my marriage. Amen.

When a Man Loves a Woman

Chapter Nine

when a
man
loves
a woman

he will wait for her

DEACON CURTIS Thomas informed me that two of our singles were living together. He went to make a home visit and saw both of their names on the mailbox. When he inquired, they replied that they were indeed "shacking." Deacon Thomas shared what the Scriptures say about such an arrangement, only to be told it was not his business.

At Christ Bible Church we practice church discipline and inform every person who attends our new members class about our accountability to each other spiritually, morally, and socially. Deacon Thomas explained that our church constitution and bylaws required him to share the situation with me. The man's response was that his living situation was none of my business either.

I followed up with a call and then a visit. The couple informed me that it was a matter of finances. I informed them that it was a matter of integrity. They were to be married in four months, so their "arrangement" would not be an issue much longer. I explained that four months is too long to bring reproach on the name of Jesus Christ. I extended the offer the church board empowered me to extend, which included helping the man find other housing if he would move out until they were married. He refused, and she went along with his decision.

My parting admonition was to the wife-to-be. If he is not disciplined enough to wait until marriage to have sex, he won't be disciplined enough to abstain from finding sex elsewhere in the future, if for some reason you are unable to be intimate during the marriage.

Of course, they left the church and vowed never to return to such a "pharisaical church." Just a short nine months later, the wife attended one of our services. I was quite surprised to see her and wanted to talk with her, but she left immediately after the service.

One of our head ushers, Mother Lampkin, came to me with a message from the wife. "Tell Pastor Ford he was right! We got married. Three months later I became ill and could not have sex. My husband divorced me two months later, and now he's living with another woman! He told me he could not live with me if I was unable to meet his sexual needs."

DON'T JUMP THE FENCE!

When a man loves a woman, he waits. There is a fence around marriage called sex. If you won't stay outside the fence before marriage, you won't stay inside the fence after marriage. Don't jump the fence. God placed it there to protect you, not punish you. Don't jump the fence!

Notice what it says in Genesis 29:20–21. "And Jacob served seven years for Rachel; and they seemed unto him but a few days, for the love he had to her. And Jacob said unto Laban, Give me my wife, for my days are fulfilled, that I may go in unto her."

Jacob waited seven years and seven days. You know what his example teaches you? As Diana Ross sings, "Love isn't easy, and it can't be hurried. No matter how long, you have to wait. You just have to wait." One man said, "If you sit on the eye of a stove, one minute seems like one hour. But if a pretty girl is sitting on your lap, one hour seems like one minute." Time becomes relative. Notice what the Scripture says: to Jacob it seemed as if it were just a few days.

Now, you need to see the full picture. First, Rachel always wore a veil. The only thing Jacob ever saw was her eyes. Second, Jacob didn't know the shape of Rachel's frame, because women in Rachel's day did not wear belts around their waists. Their clothing was full, not at all formfitting but like a tent.

For seven years Jacob is on his way out to take the sheep to pasture. He goes by Rachel's tent. She loves him and he loves her.

"Jacob?"

"Hey, girl, what's going on? How you doing? Six years left to go. I'll be coming to see you."

Think about the discipline required of Jacob. He never put his hands on her, because it was against the culture for a man to touch a woman, even to hold her hand unless she was his wife. He never kissed her, and he sure never put his tongue in her mouth! He never saw any part of her body except her eyes, because her face was veiled. We'll talk about what that means in just a moment. Do you see the implication? Think that's hard on a brother? Here she is, eyes flashing every morning you're going out and coming in.

"Jacob? Jacob?"

"Five more years, girl. Three more years, girl. One more year, girl. Yeah."

He's willing to wait. You know how we say it's hard to wait? You know how we are chomping at the bit? Some of you engaged people know how hard you had to fight to keep from falling into immorality. Sometimes we get in these conversations. "You know, but we're going to get married anyway. . . . I know—but, I mean, the Lord will forgive us, you know? Because we're on our way there now, you know? . . . It's just so hard to wait."

When a Man Loves a Woman

Jacob said it just seemed like a few days. It really wasn't hard. Do you want to know why? Love is patient. Love knows how to put on the brakes. Love knows how to wait. In other words, when a man loves a woman, he's willing to wait until after they get married to live together and have sex.

Amnon was a man who found it hard to wait. In 2 Samuel 13:1–16, Scripture tells us:

> And it came to pass after this, that Absalom the son of David had a fair sister, whose name was Tamar; and Amnon the son of David loved her. And Amnon was so vexed, that he fell sick for his sister Tamar; for she was a virgin; and Amnon thought it hard for him to do anything to her.... And [his friend Jonadab] said unto him, Why art thou, being the king's son, lean from day to day? wilt thou not tell me? And Amnon said unto him, I love Tamar, my brother Absalom's sister. And Jonadab said unto him, Lay thee down on thy bed, and make thyself sick: and when thy father cometh to see thee, say unto him, I pray thee, let my sister Tamar come, and give me meat, and dress the meat in my sight, that I may see it, and eat it at her hand. So Amnon lay down, and made himself sick: and when the king was come to see him, Amnon said unto the king, I pray thee, let Tamar my sister come, and make me a couple of cakes in my sight, that I may eat at her hand. Then David sent home to

Tamar, saying, Go now to thy brother Amnon's house, and dress him meat. So Tamar went to her brother Amnon's house; and he was laid down. And she took flour, and kneaded it, and made cakes in his sight, and did bake the cakes. . . . And when she had brought them unto him to eat, he took hold of her, and said unto her, Come lie with me, my sister. And she answered him, Nay, my brother, do not force me; for no such thing ought to be done in Israel: do not thou this folly. And I, whither shall I cause my shame to go? and as for thee, thou shalt be as one of the fools in Israel. Now therefore, I pray thee, speak unto the king; for he will not withhold me from thee. Howbeit he would not hearken unto her voice: but, being stronger than she, forced her, and lay with her. Then Amnon hated her exceedingly; so that the hatred wherewith he hated her was greater than the love wherewith he had loved her. And Amnon said unto her, Arise, be gone. And she said unto him, There is no cause: this evil in sending me away is greater than the other that thou didst unto me. But he would not hearken unto her.

LOVE OR LUST

Amnon couldn't wait! He wanted to have sex with his sister Tamar, and his desire was so intense that it made him physically ill. Yet, the text says that he "loved" her. Actually, he lusted after her. What is the difference between love and lust? Love will wait, because it is patient. Second Samuel 13 helps us identify the characteristics of lust that won't wait. It is lust when:

1. Objectivity is lost. Wanting is based on the superficial, how Tamar looked outwardly and not how she was inwardly. His wanting is based on her physical appearance, not her personality (v. 1).

2. Feelings override common sense and take control . He literally got sick (v. 2).

3. You are not concerned with the facts and will not respect the boundaries. Tamar is his sister (v. 2)!

4. You are in a hurry. Amnon was vexed (v. 2).

5. You will connive to get what you want. His cousin gave Amnon a scheme to utilize to get what he wanted (vv. 4–6).

6. You will use whoever is necessary to get what you want. Amnon uses his father's influence (v. 7).

7. You use false pretenses and give into your emotions. Amnon got in bed as if he were sick, and he manipulated Tamar into baking a cake for him (vv. 7–8).

8. You have a one-track mind. Amnon thinks of himself and what he wanted and takes advantage of his sister Tamar (v. 14).

9. When satisfaction is gained, you want nothing else to do with the other person. Amnon rapes Tamar and then puts her out (v. 15b).

10. Contempt sets in. He hated her as passionately as he had loved her (v. 15).

11. You will not listen to reason. Tamar tries to convince Amnom that she is not the cause of his hatred toward her (v. 16).

Unlike Amnon, Jacob was a man who understood that when a man loves a woman, he will wait on her. Look at what the Bible says. Jacob waited patiently. He wasn't worried about time; he was worried about his testimony. He wasn't worried about resources; he was worried about Rachel's reputation. He waited patiently.

When I facilitate marriage seminars, one of the things I tell the brothers is that you are going to have to learn to wait on your wives. Okay, I'm hungry. She has been upstairs getting ready for forty-five minutes. "Baby," I call, "how long are you going to be?"

"Two minutes," she replies. Now I want to interpret that for you, gentlemen. A woman's two minutes are equal to the two minutes that we tell them are left in the game that we're watching. Don't count the time-outs or the commercials. When we tell her there are only two minutes left in the game, we know that there is at least a half hour left!

Here's a secret I learned a few years back. When I ask, "How long are you going to be, because it's time to go?" and she says, "Two minutes," I sit down, turn on the television, and get a cup of coffee, a Coke, and a smile or something! Then I wait. After a half hour, I walk to the top of the steps. I say, "Ooh, girl. You know I was sitting there hungry and I was worried about eating and about how long you were taking. But, girl, let me tell you something. Now that I look at you, it was worth the wait. I'll wait another half hour for you!"

I have learned how to wait!

WHY LOVE WAITS

Notice Genesis 29:21. Jacob waited for sexual involvement. It says, "Jacob said unto Laban, Give me my wife, for my days are fulfilled, that I may go in unto her." Jacob is saying, "I have done everything I was supposed to do, and now it is time to consummate the relationship." He waits until they're married before he expects to have sex. Let me say it again. He waits until they're married before he expects to have sex.

There are about forty-two reasons that Scripture gives to justify waiting to have sex until you are married. I am only going to highlight a few:

1. God commands us to be pure.
2. Premarital sex can make future courtship much more difficult.
3. Failing to wait strains freedom to develop strong relationships.

4. Premarital sex brings the risk of sexually transmitted diseases.
5. Premarital sex breaks your fellowship with God.
6. It can destroy self-esteem.
7. It creates problems in marriage.
8. It can produce unplanned pregnancies.
9. Premarital sexual relationships make it difficult to break up because you have had sex.
10. Sex, not love, is the basis for the relationship.
11. It causes guilt, guilt, and more guilt.
12. It will be subject to God's judgment.
13. The divorce rate is higher in marriages where there has been premarital sex than in marriages where both parties abstained.
14. Waiting brings the blessings of God.
15. Premarital sex generally leads to extramarital affairs.
16. It is a sin against your body.
17. It is a poor testimony.
18. It affects all society.

So when a man loves a woman, he will wait. He will wait for sexual involvement. Also, in verses 23 through 27, when a man loves a woman, he will patiently solve issues. This is really powerful! Here is the scenario (now tell me this is not better than a soap opera): A guy works for seven years for a woman. On his wedding night he consummates the marriage and wakes up the next morning, only to find out that it is not the woman whom he thought he wed! He goes to the father and says, "You tricked me!" The father admits his deception but claims there is a good reason, and he wants Jacob to work an additional seven years for his intended, Rachel!

Now Jacob has two wives and has worked another seven years to satisfy his obligations to Laban for Rachel's hand in marriage! Let's tell the truth. The average brother would have just shot the daddy. But no, Jacob said, "I am going to wait for Rachel." Could Jacob have insisted and said, "I don't want your other daughter. Give me my wife right now"? It might have cost him his life, but he could have made such a demand. Look at what Jacob did instead. He said, "There are some difficulties we have to work through, Rachel. I will wait and work through these issues, because I love you."

You say, "Make it practical." Okay, I will!

You want to get married now. You have finished school and started a new job. Your fiancée still has three more years of college. Can you wait until she finishes school so that she might complete some of her educational goals?

YOU REAP WHAT YOU SOW

The real essence of this story is that Jacob is going to reap what he's sown many years prior. Seven years before he met Rachel, Jacob tricked his blind father and his brother (Genesis 27–28:5). This deception committed against Jacob by Laban may be a consequence of his earlier actions. No doubt Jacob learned that you may get by, but you don't get away. The mills of God grind slowly, but they grind fine.

Esau was planning a "drive-by" on Jacob, so his mother said, "Leave and go to my brother's house for a little while." "A little while" turned out to be twenty years, because sometimes when you plant something, the law of intensification says you always get more than what you plant. That's why the Bible says, "Sow the wind and reap the whirlwind (Hosea 8:7 NIV).

Furthermore, there's always someone a little slicker than you. Jacob was a manipulator and a deceiver. Jacob goes to his uncle Laban, who wrote the book on deception and manipulation.

Jacob, no doubt, understands how his brother, Esau, felt when he swindled him out of the firstborn's birthright, since Jacob inquires of Laban, "What is this thou hast done unto me? did not I serve with thee for Rachel? wherefore then hast thou beguiled me?" (Genesis 29:25). What is it that will keep us from doing what our "natural" inclination may be? Put the shoe on your own foot. How does it feel?

When a Man Loves a Woman

Jacob pays the high price of low living. Jacob's earlier deception cost him twenty years of his life. Yet, with consequences closing in all around him, Jacob waits for Rachel. Jacob did not whine about the consequences or give up on his dream of a life with Rachel, because he knew that when a man loves a woman, he will wait for her.

The Consequences of Past Sin

If a husband commits adultery, he has been the victimizer. He is the one who is wrong. No matter what the wife's problem is, the responsibility lies with her husband. Her reaction is a consequence of his misbehavior. If she starts to treat him poorly, the husband is the one who initiated the problem, so he must take responsibility and work it through until she no longer feels victimized and is able to extend trust again. How long does it take?

I attended a Moody Bible Institute Pastors' Conference where the instructor shared, "If you have been the perpetrator in an affair, you need to know that you can gauge about how long it will take your wife to forgive you by how long you were in the affair."

It seems to take a person at least as long to get over the pain as they were in the pain. That will give you brothers some idea to gauge about how rough and how long a ride you've got if you are working through this type of betrayal. It's our job if we've offended our wives in any way to go through the process of rebuilding trust and waiting patiently for them to extend it to us.

Think about it . . .

1. Jacob certainly waited for Rachel longer than most men might. As an unmarried man, how long were you willing to wait faithfully for the woman whom you love?
2. Did you consider the cost of engaging in sex before marriage so there would be no reproach on the name of our Lord and Savior Jesus Christ? Why or why not?
3. Why is it important to God and to your mate that you were willing to wait on her?
4. What can a man do to fend off his sexual desires prior to marriage? How would you explain your answer to a single man?

Live by it . . .

Dear Lord,

I come to You, confessing my sins and ask that You would cleanse me of my selfish ways. My desire is to live a life that is pleasing to You even when I find myself in difficult situations. However, I cannot do it alone. Teach me how to surrender to You and wait patiently so that my actions line up with Your Word. Amen.

When a Man Loves a Woman

Chapter Ten

when a
man
loves
a woman ... he weds her

WHEN A MAN loves a woman, he will work to be with her.
Notice what Genesis 29:15–18 says: "And Laban said unto Jacob,
Because thou art my brother, shouldest thou therefore serve me for
nought? tell me, what shall thy wages be? And Laban had two
daughters: the name of the elder was Leah, and the name of the
younger was Rachel. Leah was tender eyed; but Rachel was beautiful and well favoured. And Jacob loved Rachel; and said, I will
serve thee seven years for Rachel thy younger daughter."

Don't miss this! Laban is rich. I imagine in the vernacular of
today Laban would ask, "What kind of salary do you want?" A

typical contemporary young man may respond: "Well, give me $70,000 a year, a nice 401(k) plan, and profit sharing. I want a part in the business, a company car, and a private office."

That's not what Jacob said. "Give me Rachel. I want to work for Rachel's hand in marriage."

So he worked seven years for Rachel and seven years for Leah, right? Wrong. He worked fourteen years for Rachel! The working that we looked at in chapter 4 was accomplished before Jacob got married. In that work he acknowledged Rachel as a woman and proved that he understood how to treat a lady. That took one afternoon.

Jacob is working to prove he's willing to make a lifelong commitment. He has declared his love for Rachel and established a course to make her his wife. It required fourteen years—seven years before he could marry Rachel, and seven more years of working for Laban after marriage (Genesis 29:26–30). But for fourteen years he hung in there. Why? Because he wanted Rachel to be his wife.

In order to marry in Jacob's culture, you had to have some things established before you even approached your prospective wife's father. These are consistent with the order God established with Adam. First, He gave Adam work (Genesis 2:15). Second, God gave Adam specific instructions on how to live in his world, and finally God gave Adam a wife. I tell single women, if a man doesn't have a job, don't marry him. If he has no means to provide for himself, how can he provide for her? In fact, I refuse to officiate at weddings if the man does not have a job.

A FATHER PROVIDES PROTECTION AND ACCOUNTABILITY

I want you to know that Jacob worked for her by working through. He worked through every requirement that Laban demanded of him. Don't miss this principle. Jacob was willing to deal with Rachel's daddy. I believe this with all my heart. A young woman who is on her way to be married ought to have passed her intended by her dad.

Ladies, please pay special attention to the text. It says in verse 12, "And Jacob told Rachel that he was her father's brother, and that he was Rebekah's son." Rachel did not run and tell her girlfriends, or the people at church. She ran and told her father!

Let your father analyze any man who is trying to step to you. There is protection in this for you. Your dad isn't going to go for the things you see in a man. Your boyfriend is telling you how beautiful your eyes are . . . Your dad is going to look *him* dead in the eye and assess his character. Your father will perceive what kind of man he is.

The Father: Covenant Initiator

Back in that day it was widely known and accepted that men had to pay a dowry to marry. Actually, it was more than compensation to make up for the daughter's lost contribution to the household, since she would be working in her own household. The primary purpose of the dowry was for the groom to demonstrate to his prospective in-laws his ability to care and provide for their daughter.

Well, in Ghana, West Africa, this practice still exists today. Pastor Raphael, whom I met on a mission trip, showed me his dowry list. He had to provide what was asked for by each member of his fiancée's family. I asked him how long he thought it would take to amass their requests. He told me approximately three years. Wow! He also told me that his in-laws would not permit the wedding to take place until he had provided *all* that was requested. In fulfilling the requests of his future family, Pastor Raphael demonstrated the value he placed on his future wife and reassured them that he would be capable of caring for their daughter.

This Western culture stuff has got to go. In the East you know the drill well. The marriage is established between the bride's father and the prospective groom. The two men get together. It has nothing to do with the woman, per se, because her father has the right before God to transfer authority over his daughter.

JOHNNY LINGO

I want to share with you the story of Johnny Lingo. Johnny Lingo lives in the southern islands. Years ago a man from America

114   When a Man Loves a Woman

went to these islands. He wanted to get some trinkets, artifacts, and all of that. So, he went to the village of Kenny Watti.

I went to the island of Kenny Watti to seek out someone who would be a trader to help me get the things that I had on my list. I said, "Who's the best trader on the island?"

With a smile on his face, one native said, "Without a doubt, Johnny Lingo. Johnny Lingo." And then he laughed.

I said, "Well, why are you laughing when you say his name?"

He says, "Everybody here does [laughs], because, you see, Johnny paid eight cows for his wife, Serita."

"What? Eight cows? Well, I guess there's no accounting for love," I said.

"True enough," agreed the man.

And that's why the villagers grin when they talk about Johnny. They get special satisfaction from the fact that the sharpest trader in the islands was bested by Doll Old Sam Carew.

"But how?" I inquired.

"No one knows, and everybody wonders," he said.

All the cousins were urging Sam to ask for three cows and hold out for two until he was sure Johnny would pay only one. Then Johnny came to Sam Carew and said, "Father of Serita, I offer eight cows for your daughter."

"Eight cows," I murmured. I'd like to meet this Johnny Lingo. I wanted fish. I wanted pearls. So the next afternoon I beached my boat at Nurabundi, the island that Johnny lived on. I noticed as I asked directions to Johnny's house that his name did not bring the sly smile to the lips of his fellow Nurabundians as it did those on Kenny Watti. Then I met the slim, serious young man. He welcomed me with grace to his home. I was glad that from his own people he had respect unmingled with mockery.

We sat in his house and talked. Then he asked, "You come here from Kenny Watti?"

"Yes," I said.

"They speak of me on that island?" he asked.

"They said there's nothing that I might want that you can't help me get," I said.

He smiled gently. "My wife is from Kenny Watti."

"Uh, yes, I know," I said.

"They speak of her?" he asked.

"Uh, a little."

"Well, what do they say?"

"Why, just uh . . ." The question caught me off balance. "Uh, they told me you were married at festival time."

"Nothing more?" The curve of his eyebrows told me he knew there had to be more.

When a Man Loves a Woman

"Well, they also say that the marriage settlement was eight cows, and . . ." I paused.

"They wonder why? They asked that?" His eyes lighted with pleasure. "Everyone in Kenny Watti knows about the eight cows."

I nodded. "Yes, they do."

He said, "Well, in Nurabundi everybody knows it too." His chest expanded with a satisfaction as he said, "Always and forever when they speak of marriage settlements, it will be remembered that Johnny Lingo paid eight cows for Serita."

So that's the answer, I thought. *Vanity. Pride.*

Then I saw her. I watched her enter the room to place flowers on the table. She stood still a moment to smile at the young man beside me. Then she went swiftly out again. She was the most beautiful woman I've ever seen in my life! The lift of her shoulders, the tilt of her chin, the sparkle of her eyes all spelled a pride to which no one could deny her the right. I turned back to Johnny Lingo and found him looking at me.

"You admire her," he murmured.

"She's glorious. But she can't be Serita from Kenny Watti," I said.

He said, "There's only one Serita. Perhaps she does not look the way they told you she looked in Kenny Watti. She doesn't."

"I'm sorry, but I heard she was homely. They all make fun of you because you let yourself be cheated by Sam Carew."

"Do you think eight cows was too much for that woman?" he asked, as a smile slid over his lips.

"No, but how can she be so different?"

"Do you ever think," he asked, "what it must mean to a woman to know that her husband has settled on the lowest price for which she can be bought? And then later when the women talk they boast of what their husbands paid for them. One says four cows, another maybe six. How does the woman feel, the woman who was sold for one or two? This could not happen to my Serita."

"Then you did this just to make her happy?"

"Yes. I wanted Serita to be happy, but I wanted more than that. You say she is different. That is true. Many things change a woman. Things that happen inside, things that happen outside. But the thing that matters most is what she thinks about herself. In Kenny Watti, Serita believed she was worth nothing, so she acted like nothing and she looked like nothing. Now she knows she is worth more than any other woman on every island."

"Then you wanted—" He cut me off.

"I wanted to marry Serita. I loved her and no other woman."

"But . . ." I interrupted. I was close to understanding.

"But," he finished softly, "I wanted an eight-cow wife."

Listen, this man working for this woman does not apply practically in our culture. We don't work for our women. But the principle is true and should be true in our culture as well.

What are you saying, Pastor? I'm saying that what this man did was prove to his bride how valuable she was to him before he got married. Also, he established that he was somebody who was worthy to marry.

What does a man communicate when he works for a woman? You are valuable. I want you to know that there's no other man who will value you above the way I value you. Therefore, if I have to deal with your family for fourteen years just to walk you down the aisle, I love you enough and value you enough and want to spend the rest of my life with you enough to work through and devote the time.

You see, what we need is individuals who will wait to marry until they can resolve problems that have the potential to shipwreck. If I have to deal with your family—perhaps they don't like me—I'll win your family in order to win you. If you've got problems because of a previous relationship you were in, we'll work through those. Perhaps you got dogged out and kicked to the curb; then I'll do whatever it takes to help you heal. We'll get counseling. We'll do whatever it takes. I want you to know how valuable you are to me—I'll work for you because I want an eight-cow wife. Jacob worked fourteen years for Rachel because he wanted an eight-cow wife.

THE HUSBAND: COVENANT RESPONDER

Do you know why the groom's family sits on one side of the church and the bride's on the other at a wedding? This is to symbolize the covenant relationship that the couple, as well as their families, are about to enter into. In Jacob's day an animal would be slain, cut in half diagonally. The two halves would be separated and the covenant participants would walk in between the halves, stepping in the blood. In Genesis 15:9–17, this picture is given to Abraham. In this case the covenant was unconditional, because only Yahweh walked through the sacrifice.

In marriage, the bride's father is the covenant initiator and the groom is the covenant responder. That is why the groom does not walk down the aisle. The father brings his daughter down the aisle because he is her authority. When the preacher asks, "Who gives this woman to this man?" and the father says, "I do," it symbolizes transference of authority. His daughter will no longer be under his authority but under a new covenant authority, her husband. The first sign that the wife comprehends and accepts this is the voluntary acceptance of her husband's last name by adopting it as her own.

When a Man Loves a Woman

"God made he him; Male and female created he them; and blessed them, and called *their* name Adam" (Genesis 5:1–2, italics added).

A Father Continues to Provide Accountability

Before I was saved, I had a gambling problem. I used to leave work and go to Jimmy Giles, the local gambling house every Friday after I got paid. Sometimes I would lose all of my money; sometimes I would win. Some of you know what I mean. You are playing the lottery!

Anyway, I told my wife I would not gamble anymore. Yet there I was, sitting in the gambling house at three o'clock in the morning. Suddenly, there was a knock at the door. Jimmy Giles got his gun and went to the door. (It's a gambling house, so he got his gun, then went to the door!) Before I knew it, two big hands were resting on my shoulders, practically covering them. I looked up and said, "Hey pops," to my father-in-law who had just arrived.

He said, "Sonny Man," that's what he called me, "Sonny Man . . ."

Now you need to understand that I dated my wife for eight years before we got married. And in eight years I bet you my father-in-law had not said ten words to me, during the entire eight years! I heard that man talk more that evening than I had ever heard him talk.

"Sonny Man," he said, "my daughter is at home crying. Let's go."

I said, "Oh. Let me finish this hand."

"Let's go. If I tell you one more time, you're going to be sorry."

I said, "I got to go."

He started talking from the time I left my seat at the card table.

"My daughter is at home crying, and I'm going to tell you this, and you better listen to me." I was walking ahead of him more than an arm's length.

"Sonny Man," he continued, "if my daughter ever has to call me to get you again, we're going to find out how much of a man you really are."

When I got home, I put my key in the door and found my wife standing in the middle of the floor with my son crying.

We sat on the couch, and I shriveled up like a piece of bacon.

Her father said, "Baby, here he is. Now I'm going to let you two work this out. And, sweetheart, let me tell you something. If you need me, you got my number. If you ever have this situation again, you call me. He already knows what we're going to do about it."

If you ever meet my wife, ask her if I ever went back to Jimmy Giles or if I ever had a gambling problem after that night. I was "saved" before I got saved from gambling. Leslie's daddy scared the gambling out of me!

AFTER THE CEREMONY

When a man loves a woman, he will work for her by working through the things that are keeping him from her, and he will work for her by working with the situations that present themselves to disrupt their relationship. Jacob is not living in the same tent as Rachel right now. Everything that happens in Genesis 29 is from afar. When you look at chapter 30, verses 1 and 2, Jacob has joined his wife in the tent.

How many of you know that what you see is not always what you get? I like what Tony Evans says: "You don't know what you got before you get married and you go to Steak and Ale. You sit down, and you're looking across at each other. She's all made up. She's demure and petite, and she's talking real soft, and the conversation is real good. That's not what you really got. That's not what you really have. See, once you get married, you'll find out what you really have."

Anybody who is married will tell you there's a honeymoon stage. That's when you can't keep your eyes off of each other. You can't keep your hands off of each other. Guess what? The honeymoon stage ends. When the honeymoon stage ends, the real work of marriage starts. Most people think they've been tricked. They've been hoodwinked. They've been bamboozled. They have not. They need to understand that things were done in order to impress and win each other. You spent money that you normally wouldn't spend. You had conversations that you normally wouldn't have. You did all of those things. Then, after a few months of marriage, you changed. Why would you think she would not change? We get comfortable after we get to know each other. It's then that we realize the real work starts when the eyelashes come off. The real work starts when the wig comes off. The real work starts when the weave is gone. The real work starts when you understand that this individual you are hooked up with is not all that she seemed to be in the dating and the honeymoon stage, but neither are you. That's when the real work starts.

What If There Is No Ceremony?

That's what's wrong with shacking. It furthers an illusion. People who think that they can find out what a person is like without making a commitment are only fooling themselves. Living with someone is a setup because an individual will always change after you get married. It sets you up to live as married singles. Living together before marriage creates an illusion where oneness is undermined. The "you pay this bill, and I'll pay that bill" and "this is yours, and that is mine" mentality sets in. If that's in your marriage, I'm telling you, you need to begin to get counseling to work through this issue, because the Bible says, "Two shall become one."

"And Jacob did so, and fulfilled her week: and he gave him Rachel his daughter to wife also." (Genesis 29:28)

Jacob finally marries Rachel! A man who loves a woman will

wed before any sexual encounter. Jacob is able to conclude, "Listen, Rachel. You are going to be my partner in sickness and health, poverty and wealth, 'til death do us part. I realize you are the one whom God has for me for all the rest of my days. I understand that we will come together and consummate our marriage, and we'll have children, because God wants us to procreate. We'll have pleasure, because that's the second reason God gave us marriage."

Men, you must understand all of this and recognize that marriage is designed to show the world what a family ought to be. Through our unity and commitment to each other, we become a picture of Christ's relationship to His church.

Like Jacob, I have come to understand all of these things. When a man loves a woman, he marries her.

Think about it . . .

1. Should a woman be ready to marry a man if he doesn't have the proper plans in place to provide for her before the marriage? Why or why not?

2. Jacob had what it takes to ask Rachel's father for her hand in marriage. As a single man, did you believe that you were prepared to approach your intended's father or family members to ask for her hand in marriage?

3. Did you discover after you were married that you didn't marry the person you thought you were marrying? Are

you willing to share your experience with a male friend who is contemplating marriage? Explain.

4. Since you and your mate have had the opportunity to become intimately aware of each other's personalities, have you determined that you are going to make your marriage work? Why or why not?

Live by it . . .

Dear Lord,
Thank You for the blessing that my mate has brought into my life. Please open my eyes to truly understand how valuable she is in Your eyes. My ultimate prayer is to become the devoted husband You have called me to be. Amen.

when a man loves *a woman*

he warns her

And when Rachel saw that she bare Jacob no children, Rachel envied her sister; and said unto Jacob, Give me children, or else I die. And Jacob's anger was kindled against Rachel.
—Genesis 30:1–2

JACOB'S ANGER IS righteous indignation, according to Ephesians 4:26. Jacob's anger is understandable at this juncture because unrealistic expectations are being placed upon him. Ephesians 4:26 indicates sometimes anger is not sin, but we need to be careful how we handle it. There are times when there ought to be anger—a righteous indignation. Now notice what Jacob said: "Am I in God's stead, who has withheld from thee the fruit of the womb?"

I want to paraphrase Jacob's statement. It's like he's telling Rachel, "I can only do what I can do! Everything that God has given me as a responsibility in my power to do as your husband, I am going to do. When your expectations are beyond my ability to fulfill, I will let you know." Simply put, Jacob is saying, "Opening and closing the womb is God's job, not mine. Before you begin to place unrealistic expectations on me that only God can fulfill, let me get you straight."

Only Jesus

John Eldredge uses Eve to represent all women when he states, "No human being can fulfill all the longings of any other person's heart:

> There is emptiness to Eve after the Fall, and no matter how much you pour into her she will never be filled. This is where so many men falter. Either they refuse to give what they can, or they keep pouring and pouring into her and all the while feel like a failure because she still needs more. "There are three things that are never satisfied," warns Agur son of Jakeh, "four things that never say, 'Enough!' the grave, the barren womb, land, which is never satisfied with water, and fire, which never says, 'Enough!'" The barrenness of Eve you can never hope to fill. She needs God more than she needs you, just as you need Him more than you need her! So what do you do? Offer what you have.[18]

How unfair would it be if my wife said to me, "You need to be more like Pastor Mike!" I can't be like Pastor Mike. Pastor Mike is Pastor Mike. I am Pastor Ford. I have a personality. God has given it to me. I cannot be what you want me to be if what you want is for me to be like some other man, because I'm not that other man. I'm this man. If I earn thirty thousand dollars a year, don't look for a sixty-thousand-dollar lifestyle. That's far beyond what is expected. You can apply the principle in every area and every capacity. The Bible says that when a man loves a woman, he will warn her not to have unrealistic expectations. I can only be who I am.

Conclusion

THE CHINESE WANTED to protect their country from invasion. They decided to build a wall so high their enemies could not climb over it, so deep they could not dig beneath it, so wide they could not dig through it, and so long they could not get around it. In all the centuries of its long history, this Great Wall of China has only been breached three times. Guess what? The enemies didn't go over, through, under, or around the Great Wall. Each time they were invaded, it was because the enemy bribed a gatekeeper.

There is a wall, a standard that God has for a relationship between a man and a woman. He designed it to be impenetrable. The foundation is Jesus Christ. No one can go around it because it's so wide. The wall is too low to get under. Men are the gatekeepers. What value do you place on the safety of the city? That's the question I am asking. What value do we as men place on our mothers, wives, daughters, girlfriends, female companions, associates, and friends?

I submit to you that if we test the climate of our society, we will see that what's going on is not an action but a reaction. Women have had to react to the misuse and abuse by those who are supposed to esteem, value, and honor them! Some of the gatekeepers have been bribed! Now we must cope with the consequences of catastrophes we have created. As men we must rectify the wrong.

TIMELESS PRINCIPLES
FOR SUCCESSFUL LIVING

Some of you are saying that this is old-fashioned. I want you to know that godliness never goes out of style. The principles of God will never go out of style. God is saying that a man ought to be a man, and a woman ought to be a woman. Men ought to do what God designed them to do, and women likewise.

Genesis 29 affirms what God has done in creation. God is calling men to be Jacobs. Most of what Jacob did, he accomplished before Rachel became his wife. Jacob respected Rachel as a woman, and like Jacob, men need to affirm the identity, security, activity, and femininity of women in our society. Will you be a Jacob, my brother?

As men we must make a commitment to the women in our lives, before almighty God, to start today to rectify the wrongs. We must say to the Lord, "As You empower us, we will be like Jacob. We will demonstrate a Christlike love to women who are our

When a Man Loves a Woman

wives, mothers, daughters, fiancées, and friends. We know that the glue that holds the family, the church, and society-at-large together is men. Lord, we come before You today broken and repentant, asking that 1 John 1:9 would be applicable in our lives. We are not saying that we are totally messed up, but we are saying that there are areas where we can improve in regard to the love we have for our women.

"And so as a testament, we commit to the fact that we are going to meet with our wives, daughters, friends, and family to try and rectify any wrongs. We want to restore emotions and relationships that have been damaged. We want to restore the material provisions that may have been taken away. We want to rectify as much as we can, knowing we can't do anything unless You empower us. So, Lord, fill us with Your Holy Spirit so that He who is resident will become president, and empower us so that we would have a change of character, conduct, and conversation. So much so that our wives, mothers, daughters, and friends will be converted. We thank You, O Lord, for the privilege to stand and make this pledge.

"Thank You in advance for granting our request.

"We pray these things in Jesus' name,

"Amen."

Think about it . . .

1. Are you feeling as though your mate expects more of you than you are currently able to do? Be honest and share with her if you believe that some of her expectations are unrealistic.
2. Are you willing to give your mate the benefit of the doubt and reassure her that you are committed to following God's direction for you and your family?
3. Have you studied God's Word to determine the role of a man as it applies to his wife and his family?
4. Have you studied God's Word to determine the role of a woman as it applies to her husband and her family?

Live by it . . .

Dear Lord,

Through my eyes of faith, I am relying on You to help me right any wrongs that may have occurred in my marital relationship. In my duties and responsibilities, I pray that You will empower me to take my rightful place as the head of our household. To Your honor and glory, help my wife and I depend on You to fulfill the roles You have given us. Amen.

When a Man Loves a Woman

Notes

1. Susan Harter, "Causes and Consequences of Low Self-Esteem in Children and Adolescents," in *Self-Esteem: The Puzzle of Low Self-Regard,* ed. R. F. Baumeister (New York: Plenum, 1993), 95–96.

2. Karen Lee-Thorp and Cynthia Hicks, *Why Beauty Matters* (Colorado Springs: NavPress, 1997).

3. New Testament writers sometimes used these words in ways that didn't fit these precise categories, but there are New Testament scholars who interpret these words using the aforementioned distinctions. See *Vines Expository Dictionary of Old and New Testament Words*, p 382. See Dr. Kenneth S. Weust's (former Greek professor at Moody Bible Institute) *Treasures from the Greek New Testament for the English Readers*, p 57–60. See Dr. Fred R. Hughes, *Gospel of John*, p 473, Crossing Books.

4. Edith Deen, *All the Women of the Bible* (San Francisco: Harper, 1988), 29.

5. John Eldredge, *Wild at Heart* (Nashville, Thomas Nelson, 2001), 16.

6. Lee-Thorp and Hicks, *Why Beauty Matters.*

7. Gary Smalley and John Trent, *The Gift of the Blessing* (Nashville: Thomas Nelson, 1993).

8. Harvey Richard Schiffman, *Sensation and Perception: An Integrated Approach* (New York: John Wiley & Sons, 1982), 107.

9. Dolores Krieger, "Therapeutic Touch: The Imprimatur of Nursing," *American Journal of Nursing* (May 1975): 784.

10. *UCLA Monthly*, Alumni Association News (March–April 1981), 1.

11. The Complete Biblical Library, Old Testament Study Bible, Book of Genesis, World Library Press, p 32–33.

12. Dr. Myles Munroe, *Understanding the Purpose and Power of a Man* (Kensington, PA.: Whitaker House, 2002), 221.

13. John Eldredge, *Wild at Heart*.

14. Hazel Felleman, ed., *The Best Loved Poems of the American People* (New York: Doubleday, 1936).

15. Willard F. Harley Jr., *His Needs, Her Needs* (Grand Rapids: Revell, 1988), 32.

16. Dennis Rainey, *Lonely Husbands, Lonely Wives* (Dallas: Word, 1989).

17. John Powell, *Why Am I Afraid to Tell You Who I Am?* (Grand Rapids: Zondervan, 1999).

18. Eldredge, *Wild at Heart*, 189.

When a Man Loves a Woman

Bibliography

Brand, Dr. Paul, and Philip Yancey. *The Gift of Pain: Why We Hurt and What We Can Do about It.* Grand Rapids: Zondervan, 1997.

Eldredge, John. *Wild at Heart: Discovering the Secrets of a Man's Soul.* Nashville: Thomas Nelson, 2001.

Harley, Willard F., Jr. *His Needs, Her Needs: Building an Affair-Proof Marriage.* Grand Rapids: Revell, 1988.

Harter, Susan. "Causes and Consequences of Low Self-Esteem in Children and Adolescents," in *Self-Esteem: The Puzzle of Low Self-Regard,* ed. R. F. Baumeister. New York: Plenum, 1993.

Krupp, Joanne. *Woman: God's Plan Not Man's Tradition.* Salem, OR: Preparing the Way Publishers, 1999.

Lee-Thorp, Karen, and Cynthia Hicks. *Why Beauty Matters.* Colorado Springs: NavPress, 1997.

Munroe, Dr. Myles. *Understanding the Purpose and Power of Men: A Book for Men and the Women Who Love Them.* New Kensington, PA: Whitaker House, 2001.

Pride, Mary. *The Way Home: Beyond Feminism, Back to Reality.* Westchester, IL: Crossway, 1985.

Rainey, Dennis. *Lonely Husbands, Lonely Wives: Rekindling Intimacy in Every Marriage.* Dallas: Word, 1989.

Reece, Colleen L. *Women of the Bible. Fifty Biographical Sketches of Biblical Women.* Uhrichsville, OH: Barbour and Company, 1996.

Schiffman, Harvey Richard. *Sensation and Perception: An Integrated Approach.* New York: John Wiley & Sons, 1982.

Seamands, David A. *Living with Your Dreams: Let God Restore Your Shattered Dreams.* Wheaton, IL: Victor Books, 1990.

Smalley, Gary, and Trent, John. *The Gift of the Blessing.* Nashville: Thomas Nelson, 1993.

Yorkey, Mike, ed. *Growing a Healthy Home.* Brentwood, TN: Wolgemuth & Hyatt, 1990.

WHEN A WOMAN
LOVES A MAN

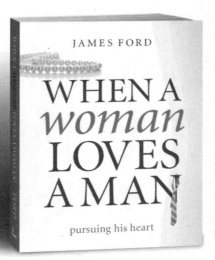

ISBN-13: 978-0-8024-6837-6

In *When a Woman Loves a Man*, through various examples, Pastor James Ford Jr. outlines the importance of a woman respecting, protecting, and caring for her mate's heart. This book, along with *When a Man Loves a Woman*, will equip those who are married and those preparing for marriage in pursuing each other's heart.

LEVB
LIFT EVERY VOICE BOOKS

Seven Reasons Why
God Created Marriage

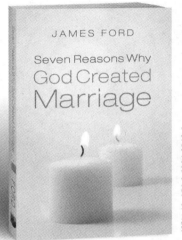

ISBN-13: 978-0-8024-2262-0

In *Seven Reasons Why God Created Marriage*, Pastor James Ford, a seasoned marriage counselor, walks readers through the Bible and shows you seven purposes for which God created marriage. This exploration will reveal timeless truths upon which readers—whether engaged or newly married—can build a solid foundation and strengthen the pillars of their marriage, reaping the benefits God intended along the way.

LEVB
LIFT EVERY VOICE BOOKS